Handmade Packaging Workshop

HANDMADE PACKAGING WORKSHOP
Copyright © 2012 RotoVision.

Manufactured in China. All rights reserved. No other part of this book may be
reproduced in any form or by any electronic or mechanical means including
information storage and retrieval systems without permission in writing from
the publisher, except by a reviewer, who may quote brief passages in a review.
Published by HOW Books, an imprint of F+W Media, Inc., 10151 Carver Road
Suite # 200, Blue Ash, Ohio 45242, (513) 531-2690. First edition.

For more excellent books and resources for designers,
visit www.howdesign.com.

16 15 14 13 12   5 4 3 2 1

Distributed in Canada by Fraser Direct
100 Armstrong Avenue
Georgetown, Ontario, Canada L7G 5S4
Tel: (905) 877-4411

Library of Congress Cataloging-in-Publication Data

ISBN 10: 1-4403-2120-5
ISBN 13: 978-1-4403-2120-7

Art Director: Emily Portnoi
Commissioning Editor: Isheeta Mustafi
Design concept: Emily Portnoi
Cover design: Emily Portnoi
Artworking and layout: rehabdesign

Handmade Packaging Workshop

Tips & Techniques for Creating Custom
Bags, Boxes & Containers

Rachel Wiles

Cincinnati, Ohio
www.howdesign.com

CONTENTS

INTRODUCTION

There is something about a brown paper package tied up with string that is immediately warm and inviting, something that makes the anticipation of discovering what is inside a little greater. As you look at the loop of the string's bow, the slightly off-kilter knot with, perhaps, a small smudge from someone's fingertip, you can almost imagine their hands taping the paper and tying the bow with care. Whatever is inside is probably wonderful, perhaps even spectacular... And this feeling is evoked because the evidence of someone's hands is all over the package.

This book explores the best and most unique "brown paper packages" that have been, in some way, touched or influenced by the element of the handmade. From labels and boxes to bags and fabrics, we'll explore a variety of hand finishes, handmade elements, manual printing processes, and techniques that push these projects beyond the ordinary realm of packaging into something truly special.

KEY

 HANDMADE

 HANDMADE ELEMENTS REPRODUCED MECHANICALLY

 HANDMADE AESTHETIC

 HANDMADE ELEMENTS

 HAND-FINISHED

BASICS

This section focuses on design considerations. In it I provide a brief overview of the packaging fundamentals that should serve as the sturdy platform of knowledge upon which you begin every package design. After all, how effective is a lovely package design if you've completely underestimated crazy shipping costs or forgotten to take into account the longer turnaround time for letterpress printing? We'll look at some of the basics of package design, some tools that will be absolutely necessary (and some that, while not imperative, are fun to use), packaging materials, methods of printing, printing and shipping logistics, and that ever-present buzzword, sustainability.

PACKAGING ELEMENTS

We take a close look at specific packaging components in this section. We'll delve into some of the loveliest handmade packaging around. All of the packaging showcased involves some sort of handmade element or aesthetic. For clarity's sake, each project bears one or more icons to denote the level of hand-involvement in that project. (You'll find a key to these icons on the page opposite.) I've selected particularly intriguing projects as case studies, wherein we'll examine the designer's or studio's ideation and creation process and the finished result on a deeper level.

REUSABLE ELEMENTS

This section focuses on sustainable, recycled, upcycled, or reusable packaging, from fabric wraps to candle holders made from wine bottles. Considering the fragile environment in which we live has become of major importance. While we've seen plenty of "greenwashing" on a corporate level in the world of consumer products, I believe that most designers are truly concerned with sustainability and are growing increasingly conscientious and selective in their choice of packaging materials and processes in regard to how it will affect the environment. From soy ink to paper pulp, we're given an increasing variety of earth-friendly tools to use for our packaging products.

GOING PRO

Going Pro focuses on a selection of designers whose designs are peppered throughout these pages, and how they work. Inevitably, when I pick up a book on package design, I flip through the glossy photos, then scour the pages for information on the designers and studios featured within. I love learning about a designer's or studio's process: what makes them tick, what printing methods they love, their favorite packaging project. Every designer and studio is different. With a range of varying viewpoints, design processes, and inspirations, hopefully some will resonate with you.

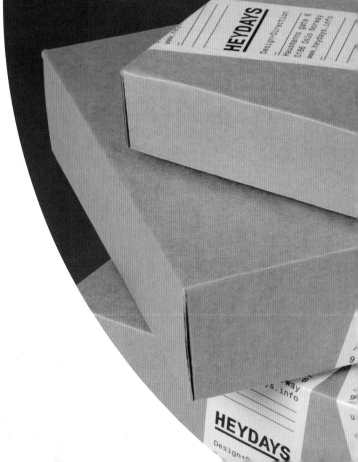

DESIGN
CONSIDERATIONS
BASICS

CHAPTER 1 TOOLS AND EQUIPMENT

Whether you're a seasoned pro or a packaging novice, there are some essential tools you'll need to acquire for your packaging and design needs, as well as some items that, while not necessary, can provide you with added avenues of creativity.

PRINTER

If you are a freelance or novice designer working from home, it's essential to have a decent printer or two for mock-ups. If it's in your budget, I would recommend at least two printers: one low-cost printer for everyday tasks, such as printing out schedules and contracts, and one upscale printer for design mock-ups, presentations, and so on. For the everyday printer, select an all-in-one printer from HP, Canon, Kodak, or Epson, allowing you to print, scan, and copy items using one machine. For your big-ticket printer, I recommend a color laser printer or a large-format inkjet printer. Canon, Epson, and HP are respectable and reliable makes. There is an endless variety of ever-changing options, so I suggest researching printers based on your particular needs and specifications. User reviews will prove invaluable.

If you can afford to go big, a larger-format color laser printer can cost upwards of $5000. This expenditure is typically only justified in very busy studios or firms.

CUTTING TOOLS

X-acto knives

Invaluable for a variety of projects, X-acto knives are especially useful for making precise cuts for package dieline mock-ups. Buy a bunch, in a range of sizes, with a lot of extra blades—you'll be glad you did. If you've been designing long enough, you've probably also taken off a bit of finger on more than one occasion! X-actos are incredibly sharp, so be careful. It wouldn't hurt to keep a box of band-aids nearby, too.

Cutting mat and rulers

A self-healing cutting mat is an absolute necessity for all the cutting and measuring you do as a designer. Buy the largest size you can. It will make many jobs much easier. You'll also need a selection of rulers. Metal rulers allow for precision cutting and also provide a bit of a barrier between you and the X-acto knife's blade. Cork-backed rulers that won't slip are the best. I recommend having a few rulers of more than 24in (61cm) long.

1.

1. X-acto knives will prove invaluable when you are developing packaging products. Many designers have a selection scattered about their workspace alongside pens and pencils.

SOFTWARE

I recommend the Adobe suite of design software (InDesign, Illustrator, and Photoshop). It is the industry standard. If you are a student, look for discounts on Adobe products with the numerous online academic vendors.

EXTRAS

Screenprinting set-up

You can go down to a hobby shop and buy a basic screenprinting kit, or a Google search will reveal countless tutorials on how to create your own screenprinting set-up for next to nothing, costwise. This method of printing involves a bit of learning, but is a relatively easy way to introduce the handmade aesthetic to your designs.

The Gocco printer is a Japanese color screen-printing system that looks like a toy but can produce some amazing results. It is quick and easy to use and involves less of a learning curve than traditional screenprinting. According to SaveGocco.com, "The system works using flash bulbs, a carbon-based image or photocopy, and an emulsion-coated screen. When the bulbs are manually flashed, the carbon in the drawing or photocopy burns the screen into a stencil. Several colors of ink can then be applied at one time and multiples can be stamped out, as many as 100 before re-inking is needed. Fans of Print Gocco appreciate its size, cleanliness, relatively inexpensive cost, and the fact that several colors can be printed in one pass."

Here's the caveat—Riso, the manufacturer of Gocco, shipped its last stock of supplies to vendors and closed its doors on Gocco in 2008. However, there is a whole community of Gocco lovers and suppliers still out there, so if you're interested in learning more about Gocco or acquiring one, www.savegocco.com is a great starting point.

2.

Letterpress printing

Letterpress is truly a universe unto itself. It is the oldest printing method there is, and also one that requires a significant amount of time, devotion, practice, and patience to become a pro at, but the beautiful, tactile results are unlike those of any other printing method. I suggest doing a lot of research and taking some beginner courses on letterpress before acquiring one. A couple of good places to start your research are www.briarpress.org and www.fiveroses.org/intro.htm.

2. This Chandler & Price letterpress is a good option for letterpress enthusiasts, but is very heavy and can be pricey.

CHAPTER 2 MATERIALS AND RESOURCES

Advances in technology have made an increasing number of materials available for use in commercial packaging. Not all of these, however, lend themselves to handmade packaging or packaging that involves handmade processes. In this chapter we will look at materials that are commonly used in handmade packaging.

SELECTION CRITERIA

Before ever settling on materials for a project, you should take into consideration the following five factors, which should influence your choice:

1. The product—what is it? Will it be shipped? If so, how?

2. Storage and protection—how will the product be stored? Does it require extra protection or have special requirements, such as the need to maintain a certain temperature?

3. Your market—who is your target customer? Where should your product be sold in order to reach your target market? What kind of packaging will set your product apart so that your target market pays attention?

4. Costs and time requirements—what are the costs of the materials and processes? How long does it take to produce the packaging from start to finish? Do you need packaging that can be turned around quickly or can you afford longer production times?

5. Scalability—if you are building a small business, you should consider the scalability of your packaging. If your business experiences serious growth, are the costs and turnaround times associated with your packaging style sustainable, or will you need to redesign your packaging once factors such as increased costs and shorter production times are considered?

COMMON MATERIALS

Glass

Glass is a great packaging choice for many reasons. It is:

- recyclable
- tactile
- compatible with a great variety of printing methods and labeling technologies
- impermeable
- hygienic (great for sterile products)
- able to protect light-sensitive substances (if it's colored)
- able to keep products fresh for a long time.

The downside? It's breakable! Some types more than others.

Glass is a good packaging choice for products ranging from beverages to personal-care products. If you choose to use glass in your packaging, you'll need to give extra consideration to protecting it during shipping. Glass can also be quite heavy, which could increase your shipping costs.

The most commonly used glass is Type III, used for most soda bottles, wine bottles, perfume bottles, jars, etc. It is made from untreated commercial soda-lime glass, which has above-average chemical resistance. It is compatible with most items it might be filled with, but is not suitable for autoclaving (sterilizing through high-temperature steaming) or for freeze-dried medicines.

For pharmaceutical or chemical products that are sensitive to pH changes, there is Type I glass, which is highly resistant and releases little alkali so the pH balance is better maintained.

1. Viola Sutanto, personal project. The idea of fabric wrapping is simple. Traditional fabric wraps—furoshiki—are made of silk, but many fabrics, including cotton, rayon, and nylon, can be used.

Plastic

Plastic often gets a bad rap, but it remains a good choice for products that will be shipped long distances, that need a flexible, tear-resistant package, or that need a package that can withstand extreme temperature fluctuations. Plastic is also very lightweight and is often cheap to produce. There are six commonly used types:

1. High-density polyethylene (HDPE). This is one of the most widely used plastics out there. It is rigid and opaque, and can be used with almost every type of liquid except solvents. It is most commonly seen in milk jugs, and containers for laundry detergents, household cleaners, and personal-care products, including shampoo and conditioner.

2. Low-density polyethylene (LDPE). You'll often see this type of plastic used for clothing and food bags and as shrink- or stretch-wrap films.

3. Polyethylene terephthalate (PET). This is a clear plastic often used for water, soda, and condiments.

4. Polyvinyl chloride (PVC). You often see this used in packaging for such things as pillowcases, sheets, or comforter sets. PVC is oil-resistant and clear.

5. Polypropylene (PP). Another choice for use in bottles, this is also used for caps. It isn't as clear as PET or PVC.

6. Polystyrene (PS) This plastic has many forms with different rigidities and uses, from CD or jewel cases and pill bottles to clamshell containers for foods such as meat and eggs.

For more information on plastic's impact on the environment and the safety of using plastic from a personal health standpoint, see page 20.

Paperboard

"Paperboard" is a general term for sheets made of recycled paper stock or virgin wood fiber; these are typically manufactured by laminating several layers of paper together. There are several types of paperboard. Bleached (or SBS—solid bleached sulfate) paperboard offers excellent printing, folding, and scoring characteristics that make it a prime choice for folding cartons, milk cartons, and food containers.

Corrugated paperboard

More popularly known as cardboard, this material is often recyclable and has a multitude of packaging uses, from soap to computers.

Cans/tin

These days, cans are made of aluminum or steel and are typically embellished with a plastic or paper label glued around the outside. Cans are mainly used for food packaging, but canisters are often used in candle or confection packaging and are very affordable. Steel cans have the added bonus of being highly recyclable.

Paper pulp

Molded paper pulp is made from natural cellulose fibers, making it biodegradable and highly sustainable. Although traditionally associated with items such as box inserts, cup-carrying trays, and egg-carton packaging, paper pulp has been increasingly used by environmentally aware companies.

Cloth

From burlap and canvas to finely woven cotton, fabric is a feasible packaging option for many projects, and is typically screenprinted.

2. Aesthetic Apparatus (see page 76) designed these labels for Andrews and Dunham Damn Fine Tea. Each label for this artisan tea brand is screenprinted by hand in Aesthetic Apparatus' studio and applied to an aluminum canister.

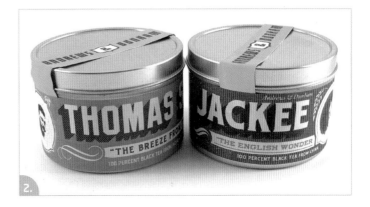

RESOURCES

Materials

Specialty Bottle
www.specialtybottle.com

This company has a huge variety of packaging (glass bottles, glass jars, tin containers, plastic bottles, plastic jars, aluminum bottles, and specialty items) in a large range of sizes. Prices are available for both small and very large quantities.

Ebottles
www.ebottles.com

Ebottles has many of the same products as Specialty Bottles but, sometimes, bottle sizes and styles vary between sites, so if you're looking for a specific size or style, it's good to take a look at a couple of different sites. This company also supplies water bottles, canning jars, fancy imported glass bottles, and glass cosmetic and perfume bottles. They price for both small and large quantities.

Molded Fiber
www.molded-pulp.com

There are no prices listed on this site, but they have a nice gallery of projects made using molded paper pulp, an incredibly eco-friendly material.

Uline
www.uline.com

Uline carries almost everything you'll ever need for shipping and also sells tags, custom labels, custom tapes, CD and DVD packaging, bags, and other custom products.

Packaging Supplies
www.packagingsupplies.com

Packaging Supplies has a good range of packaging and shipping items, and its selection of boxes is particularly good. Quantities start at 100 pieces.

Associated Bag Company
www.associatedbag.com

Another site with a variety of products, this company is most notable for its bags.

Clearbags
www.clearbags.com

Has almost any style and size of clear bag you could ever want, including compostable eco-bags.

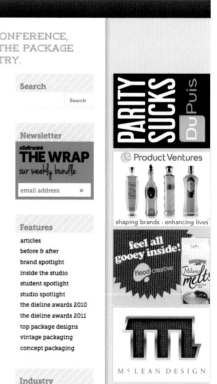

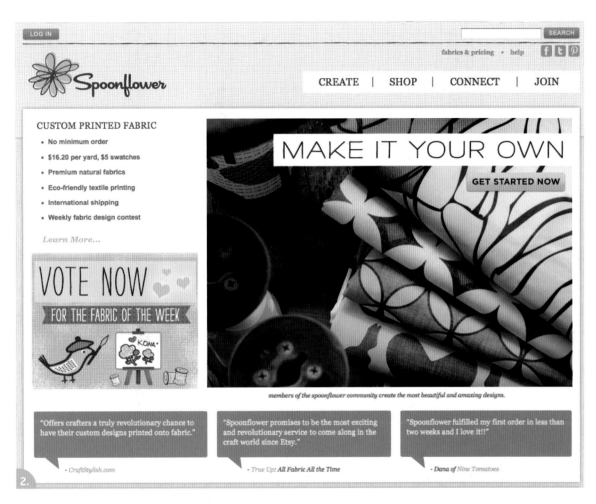

1. The Dieline website showcases innovative and successful packaging projects. This site is great for keeping up with the latest trends.

2. Spoonflower offers an easy and affordable means of having your bespoke fabric patterns printed and delivered.

Papermart
www.papermart.com
Papermart has 26,000 different products to choose from, running the gamut from soft vinyl pouches to papers and craft supplies.

Nashville Wraps
www.nashvillewraps.com
Has a nice selection of eco-friendly and natural packaging options.

Muslin Bags
www.muslinbag.com
Carries a good selection of muslin bags in a large variety of sizes.

Spoonflower
www.spoonflower.com
Upload a pattern or design to this fabric-printing site, choose from a variety of fabrics, and have your custom-created fabric delivered to your doorstep.

Design

The Dieline
www.thedieline.com
This is a great place to keep up with the latest packaging trends.

Lovely Package
http://lovelypackage.com
This site gathers inspirational examples of packaging.

Packaging of the World
www.packagingoftheworld.com
Another site that showcases packaging trends.

Sustainable Packaging
www.sustainablepackaging.org
This site is dedicated to sustainable packaging.

Packaging | UQAM
http://packaginguqam.blogspot.com/
A interesting site offering sustainable approaches to packaging.

CHAPTER 3 PRINTING AND SHIPPING

Your choice of printing method is an important decision because it will affect your overall costs, your impact upon the environment, and your turnaround times. No one shipping method or supplier will fit everyone, so it's best to do your own research and select a service that suits your product.

PRINTING

With package design you have a good set of options. You can let the printing method influence your design or go the other way around, depending on your product. Obviously, with handmade packaging we're likely to see more hands-on techniques such as letterpress and screenprinting than with commercial products.

Digital printing

Digital printing is very similar to offset, but lacks the actual plate production. Instead, all images and text remain in a digital form from creation to output. Because of this, modifications can be made easily, the turnaround time is very quick, and the process is environmentally friendly—especially if a non-polluting ink such as soy, is used. This is also a very cost-effective option. It is likely that it will be used more frequently for handmade packaging in the future as image quality continues to improve.

Offset lithography (offset printing)

This is the most popular type of printing for packaging because it provides fantastic image quality and control. Presses are either sheet or roll fed. Offset printing works on the principle that oil and water don't mix. A photochemical process is used to transfer images and text onto a plate that accepts oil-based inks and repels water. The ink adheres to the image area and the water to the non-image area. The image is then offset (transferred) to a rubber blanket, then from the rubber blanket to paper. It is called "offset" because the image is not printed directly to the paper from the plate.

New technology has allowed plates to be produced directly from computer software, rather than from films, which need to be created and then processed before being made into plates. This not only saves time and money, but is also more environmentally friendly.

1. Letterpresses come in many different vintages and sizes. This Heidelberg, at Delphine Press, is a fine example of the old and large type of press that is still in use. (Photograph by Vallentyne Photography.)

2. Letterpress printing can be a costly option due to the fact that it is a time-consuming process, and one that requires a good deal of knowledge and expertise.

Flexography (flexo)

Flexography revolves around the use of flexible relief polymer plates (an updated version of letterpress, really), which makes it a great option for almost any material and form, including plastic bags, milk cartons, and flexible film, but it is most widely used on nonporous materials used in food packaging. The polymer plate contains a raised image area that captures the ink. A cylinder rotates the plate through the machine and the ink is transferred from the plate onto the substrate. Water-based inks can be used with this process, making it a more environmentally safe option.

Letterpress

Letterpress, the oldest form of printing, enjoyed a great resurgence during the 2000s. It instantly adds a lovely tactile quality to any project. It is also a fairly costly option compared with the methods previously discussed. A metal (or, more often these days, photo-polymer) plate is created with the image or text in relief. The plate is inked and run through the press, and the ink is transferred directly to the paper or other material. One of the trademark distinctions of letterpress printing is the meeting or "kiss" of the plate and the substrate. This, depending on one's preference, can create deep impressions that can be felt with the fingertips. Because each color necessitates its own plate and its own run through the press, letterpress is most cost-effective when just one or two colors are used. It is most often seen in small runs of greeting cards,

invitations, stationery, or special-edition products such as poetry chapbooks. However, letterpress is also successfully used for high-end or luxury packaging projects.

Gravure/Rotogravure

This is one of the most expensive printing options, due to the cost of making the plates, and thus is typically reserved for large print runs with high production speeds or for high-end designs for packaging such things as art books and swanky magazines. Unlike flexography and letterpress, this process relies on etched cylinders that carry ink and transfer it to the substrate as the substrate is passed between the two cylinders. The substrate can be either sheet-fed (gravure) or roll-fed (rotogravure).

Screenprinting (silkscreening)

The easiest way to visualize this method is to think of a stencil. A fine-mesh screen is "burned" using photosensitized chemicals. Ink is then drawn across the screen and forced through the area burned by the image and onto the substrate below. This method works well on fabric, paper, plastic, wood, and metal. It is relatively inexpensive, but image detail is not as good as with other printing methods. On top of that, a different screen is required for each color; if you are printing yourself, it can be time-consuming trying to line up or register images, and this does pose some difficulties for beginners.

SHIPPING

There are many shipping options available. PackagingPrice.com has a great packaging guide that discusses shipping in detail. If the packaging design is for a large account or a client with a national presence, they are likely to have shipping logistics in place, so you can work with them directly.

For smaller or start-up businesses, the major shipping vendors, such as the U.S. Postal Service (USPS), FedEx, UPS, and DHL explain services and rates on their websites. There are also websites that will create comparison costs for the major shippers based on information you enter about your package. Try www.iship.com and also www.InterShipper.com.

Shipping vendors also have representatives who will meet with business owners to review their needs and explain options. You might be able to negotiate discounts by meeting with one.

When prepping a project for shipping, there are three things to consider:
1. the outer package, the box
2. the inner packaging, such as Styrofoam peanuts, bubblewrap, etc.
3. the sealing method

Outer packaging

There are many outer-packaging options available. Basic choices for outer packaging are:
- corrugated cardboard boxes
- corrugated mailers
- padded envelopes (padded, bubble, Tyvek®, Courier)
- Stay Flat mailers
- mailing tubes
- wooden crates
- plastic cases

Corrugated boxes are the most popular type of outer packaging because they offer good product protection, are relatively inexpensive and lightweight, and are stackable. Refer to PackagingPrice.com for an in-depth discussion regarding outer-package types and what kind of product each is suited to.

Most products will need some sort of inner cushioning for protection in addition to the outer packaging. Most major shippers will not reimburse your costs if the product is damaged and you cannot prove that the product was properly packed. The best way to ensure your product is safe is to pack it to withstand a drop from the following heights based on weight (this is called the ISTA—International Safe Transit Association—3A, 2004 test). This test was developed to evaluate the ability of a package to adequately protect an item when shipped in small-parcel distribution environments such as USPS, Fedex, etc.
- For a product weight of less than 70lb (32kg), the average expected drop height is 18ft (5.5m), while the worst-case drop height is 36ft (11m).
- For products weighing 70–150lb (32–68kg), the average drop height is 12ft (3.5m) and the worst-case scenario is 24ft (7m).

1.

1. Matches, being hazardous materials, require special packaging for mailing. (Design: Little & Company)

Inner packaging

As with outer packaging, there are many options to consider, such as:

- Bubble Wrap®
- foam wrap
- foam peanuts
- foam in place
- engineered foam
- inflatable packaging
- crumpled paper
- corrugated inserts

Again, let the product determine the material you choose. Also note that, for those companies or designers interested in recyclability and/or sustainability, some of these options will be better than others.

Sealing method

Just as important as your inner and outer packaging is your sealing method. If your package isn't properly sealed and things fall out and get damaged, all that effort you put into the packaging is worthless. Allow your package and your own sensibilities to help you determine which method will work best for you.

Tape is the most popular sealing option, but not all types are suitable for sealing packages. Pressure-sensitive tapes (which are also known as box, carton, or adhesive tapes and are typically made with a plastic backing and an adhesive side) are the most common types. "Pressure-sensitive" simply means that the tape must be applied with a small amount of pressure.

Water-activated tape is also used for sealing. The adhesive for this type of tape must first be moistened with water. This type typically incorporates fiberglass yarn which reinforces it, making it much stronger than most pressure-sensitive tapes, so less tape may be needed.

There are a few types of tape you should definitely not use in sealing packages: masking tape, duct tape, and cellophane tape.

2. When shipping these candles made from recycled wine bottles, there are a couple of considerations at play: the breakable nature of glass, keeping the candles cool so that the wax doesn't soften or melt, and the weight. (Design: Stitch Design Co.)

CHAPTER 4 SUSTAINABILITY

It was not until the twenty-first century that awareness and concern for the environment truly reached the mainstream and became an issue to be considered with every packaging project.

THE THREE Rs

"The three Rs" is a mantra that has been hammered into our cultural consciousness since the dawning of increased environmental awareness in the 1960s. During the 1980s and 1990s, many countries focused more on the growing waste problem and initiated recycling and reuse programs, though less was done to implement the first R—reduce.

In the twenty-first century, large commercial brands got in on the act, adopting more environmentally friendly practices and packaging, and making attempts to offset their carbon footprint by increasing efforts in other areas, such as replanting trees. One of the ultimate goals for sustainable packaging, however, and one that still presents challenges for many companies and designers, is creating packaging that is elevated above the traditional cradle-to-grave model to a truly environmentally friendly, closed-loop model such that the packaging is created with renewable energy, uses renewable or recycled materials, and is recycled or upcycled at the end of its usage to become something new. Thus, it never reaches the "grave" or landfill, but is looped back into a new life cycle.

According to the Sustainable Packaging Coalition (a group dedicated to promoting environmental packaging), packaging is sustainable if it:
• is beneficial, safe, and healthy for individuals and communities throughout its life cycle
• meets market criteria for both performance and cost
• is sourced, manufactured, transported, and recycled using renewable energy
• optimizes the use of renewable or recycled source materials
• is manufactured using clean production technologies and best practices
• is made from materials healthy in all probable end-of-life scenarios
• is effectively recovered and utilized in biological and/or industrial closed-loop cycles.

When you are considering the sustainability of your packaging design, keep the following options in mind.

1. Heydays, self-promotion
Design firm Heydays (see page 70) uses readily available brown boxes and a roll of stickers for a low-cost stationery option that's very recyclable and has a low environmental impact.

2.

2. Elea Lutz for Nostalgia Organics
Elea Lutz (see page 122) created the packaging for her bath and body line, Nostalgia Organics, from 100% post-consumer recycled paper.

MATERIALS

Paper, paperboard, glass, wood, plastic, aluminum, and steel can all be recycled. Newer materials, such as molded pulp—which is made of 100% recycled paper—are especially environmentally friendly (see Chapter 2 for more information). Use environmentally sourced paper: chlorine-free paper, tree-free paper (cotton, which works beautifully with letterpress), and recycled papers. Bioplastics and plant-based biodegradable cartons and bags are other good choices, especially for food items.

PRINTING

Digital printing is more environmentally friendly than other printing methods, such as offset printing (see Chapter 3 for more details), because it doesn't need the films and chemicals used in other processes. If you do choose another printing process, consider a printer that uses soy inks or vegetable-oil-based inks, and/or nontoxic toners. Please also note that some special printing processes, such as UV coating or foil stamping, will render a recyclable material such as paperboard non-recyclable, so be sure to talk with your printer before using these techniques.

REUSE

Think about making your packaging very easy for users to reuse for other things. Don't overpackage or use frivolous elements. Each element of your packaging should "earn" its place in the design.

RESOURCES

Information
Packaging Strategies
www.packstrat.com
Provider of insights, analysis, and perspectives on global packaging topics and technologies. Produces a regular newsletter and runs conferences such as the Sustainable Packaging Forum.

The Sustainable Packaging Coalition
www.sustainablepackaging.org
The Sustainable Packaging Coalition® (SPC) is dedicated to an environmental vision for packaging. Through member support, an informed approach, and supply-chain collaborations, they endeavor to build packaging systems that encourage economic prosperity and a sustainable flow of materials. The SPC is a project of GreenBlue®, a nonprofit organization that equips business with the science and resources to make products more sustainable.

PACKAGING
ELEMENTS
CASE STUDIES

CHAPTER 5 LABELS

If you're like me, you may have bought a bottle of wine more for its cool or beautiful label than for how it tastes. This chapter features many tempting wine bottles, as well other packaging projects that catch the eye, including beautifully intricate pretzel packaging, maple syrup elevated to near art-object status, and some damn finely packaged tea.

PEARLFISHER

Pearlfisher is an incredibly prolific and successful design agency that serves both the USA and the UK. It has created award-winning work for a range of clients, from Absolut Vodka to Cadbury Dairy Milk.

The Jme line was created by Pearlfisher from the ground up for renowned chef Jamie Oliver, covering all home categories from textiles to outdoor entertaining. The line reflects Oliver's relaxed approach to eating, entertaining, and enjoying life, and contains many handmade-style elements that keep the line fresh and fluid. Where possible, all packaging is 100% recyclable or recycled.

The Jme lifestyle range is an eclectic, exciting mix of food products and products for the home. The brand is generous and inspirational, celebrating personal style rather than enforcing a single aesthetic. Each unique item is sourced from artisans around the world. Packaging for each product within the food range has its own design to reflect the individual origins and qualities of the products inside.

Hand-drawn type and numbers that look as though they were printed by hand-stamping give these food items a casual, homemade feel; printing them commercially allows for production on the scale required.

1-3. Client: Jme
Hand-drawn type and numbers (electronically reproduced).

CHILLI SEA SALT

a pinch of ROSE MARY sea salt

2.

LEMON CURD .J

4 oz

of French beans in this
FRENCH BEAN RELISH

1/2 lb

of mango in this
MANGO CHUTNEY

3.

ABBY BREWSTER

Abby Brewster is a freelance designer based in Brooklyn, New York, USA. The two projects shown here were completed as student work. "In most of my projects, form really does follow function," says Brewster. "I'm a firm believer in design based on the usability and functionality of a product—understanding how a consumer interacts with a product is key to creating a meaningful experience. Both projects really have this thought process at the core of their design."

Bridge Street Fromagerie is a family-owned cheese shop located in historic Lambertville, New Jersey, USA. Brewster designed a series of dual-purpose adhesive, hand-applied labels. These secure the paper wrapping of the cheeses and provide Bridge Street Fromagerie's cheesemongers with a means of sharing knowledge with their customers. The cheesemongers write on the individual characteristics of the product along with suggested alcohol pairings.

Brewster explains, "This packaging system is part of a larger retail design concept: I looked to the other elements of the fromagerie to influence how to develop the packaging. For instance, as I aimed to create an atmosphere that encouraged customers to congregate even after making their purchases, I saw the label system as an opportunity to encourage further conversation between the shop's workers and patrons. The idea that Bridge Street would sell a large variety of cheeses and goods was at the heart of the retail concept, but this did lead to a bit of a challenge when creating a series of labels that would

be flexible enough to fit the various shapes and sizes of their products. Nothing a little research couldn't solve; countless cheese purchases later, I landed on a set of label sizes that would work whether you were packaging a wheel of Gouda or a wedge of Cheddar."

For the project opposite, Brewster focused on a chain of brewpubs, Triumph Brewing Company, located in Princeton, New Jersey; and in both New Hope and Philadelphia, Pennsylvania. Each pub only serves beers that are recently brewed in-house, so rarely does one pub have the same beer on tap as the other two locations—"great if you want to be surprised with what

you can order, not so much if you have a particular beer in mind," says Brewster.

Brewster designed this packaging system to enable each location to be provided with a selection of beers from the other brewpubs in the chain. She says, "Bottles are mass-produced and distributed to all three breweries, while the labeled tape allows each location to bottle what they are currently brewing and apply the correct labeled tape by hand. Shipping of the bottles between locations enables each brewpub to share their brews. There are, of course, some placement challenges with hand-labeling the bottles—a process that does take a few tries to get right."

1. Client: Bridge Street Fromagerie
Labels written and applied by hand.

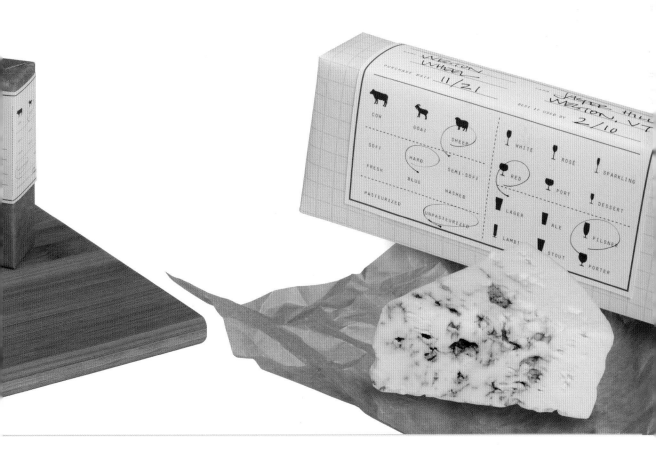

 2-3. Client: Triumph Brewing Company
Labels applied by hand.

INSITE DESIGN

Insite Design is a small agency based in Burlington, Ontario, Canada. The designers at Insite focus on solving branding and communication challenges with strategic solutions involving mixed media and tactile, interactive consumer touch points.

Creative Director Barry Imber says, "Much of our work involves execution that utilizes art and illustration within the design, as this is our love but, also, by experience, we know that this form of communication resonates with a premium consumer who values good design, hand-drawn or partially hand-drawn visuals, and well-considered products. Mostly, it's just fun."

"Five Rows makes awesome wine, by hand, the hard way," says Imber. When asked to assist the winery in creating a brand and subsequent package, Imber says it was clear that they would also go to great lengths to do as much as possible by hand. "We set out to create a brand image and package that honored this sensibility, embellished the farm spirit, would feel at home in their relaxed barn showroom environment, and would instill the rural image within the mind of the viewer. The initial brand was resolved with a simple signature rendered by hand in the studio along with watercolor and pen-and-ink sketches and abstractions. For the package, we brought these elements together within a farm-inspired layout that focused heavily on simple yet elegant type design."

1.

Costs in production were also considered, as was the time-intensity of application and finishing. Everything needed to be in a balance. Thus, Insite combined mechanical methods of production with handwriting to ensure the labels were repeatable and consistent over time, but would not lose the handmade feel, nor would they tire out the winery when it was time to label another vintage.

Another big consideration was creating hand-involved labels without falling into a low-quality, DIY, crafty aesthetic that might detract from the seriousness, quality, or value of the wine. The label had to be executed with the same level of skill as the wine itself and, as such, techniques that would result in perfection and consistency were needed to create a final package that wows while instilling trust and the expectation of quality in the consumer.

The result is an expression of what is in the bottle, as well as a tour of the winery's processes, in which customers may learn of the great depth of work, love, and dedication that goes into every bottle. Each bottle is signed by hand, on the glass, by the winemaker, then the paper is wrapped by hand around each bottle and fastened with a hidden piece of adhesive. The bottle top is dressed with a dime of black wax by hand, to protect the cork, and is further adorned with a strip of paper overwrap made from fragments of copied winemaker's field notes. The winemaker hand-numbers the bottles and adds other significant variable information to each label for that extra hand-crafted touch.

1–2. Client: Five Rows Craft Wine/Lowrey Vineyards
Hand-written labels, hand-finished.

2.

Imber describes the thinking behind another packaging project for the same client, for the product Icewine by Five Rows Craft Wine/Lowrey Vineyards. "Icewine has been traditionally marketed as a rare and highly coveted liquid to be consumed on occasion. Being lovers of the stuff, we've always believed that position should be less of occasion and more staple, and that this position could be asserted without compromise of quality or price premium— Icewine is insanely labor-intensive to create and, as such, demands a high retail price."

He continues, "It was decided that a folded, glueless piece of paper wrapped tight to the bottle with an elastic band would create a nice, hand-crafted effect. They used a flint-glass bottle, which added to the reusable milk-bottle feel of the package. The label is essentially a carrier for winemaker notes on the production of the wine as well as its origin. The initial release was digitally printed at low volume, hand-cut, and applied by hand with elastics, similar to the remaining 1000 bottles. Many of the graphics are also hand-drawn, which is consistent with the Five Rows identity. The flint bottles were finished off with a hand-drawn signature by Wes Lowrey, the winemaker."

1.

 1-2. Client: Five Rows Craft Wine/Lowrey Vineyards
Hand-drawn graphics, hand-written labels, hand-finished.

ANORIA GILBERT AND TAYLOR AHLMARK

Gilbert and Ahlmark started Maak Soap Lab during a period of post-college restlessness combined with a move to Portland, Oregon, USA. "After walking, eating, and drinking Portland for a year, we started capturing the unique Portland spirit in a bigger project—the craft of soaping," says Gilbert. "I had the basics of soaping. Combined with Taylor's hands-on design education and professional experience, a blend of old-world craft and ephemeral craftsmanship began to emerge from our soapy basement. After endless experimentation and enough practice batches to clean the city, we developed our brand and product line, and began selling soap locally in town. We've since introduced new product lines, begun private-label work with local companies, and can be found in stores both nationally and internationally."

The inspiration behind the packaging for Maak products is the idea of ephemera. "Ephemera drives our brand design—the enjoyment of what would normally be mundane and routine by focusing on quality and simple pleasures. This is reflected in our soap labels that resemble tear-away tickets, complete with hand-stamped 'best before' date," says Gilbert.

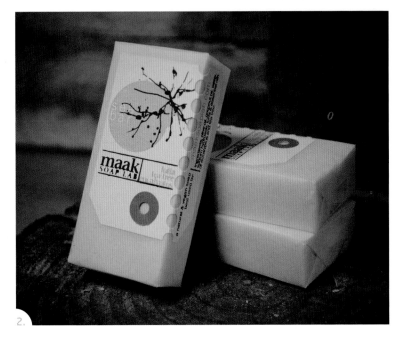

 1–4. Personal project
Screenprinting, hand-stamping, hand-assembly.

Every soap is hand-wrapped and layered with a screenprinted label, produced in-house with the soap. "This gives the package texture and depth, making it interesting to touch and examine in your hand; a sentiment that is carried through to the soap. Our essential oils are packaged in amber apothecary bottles, with stamped waxed-linen labels. We wax the labels with beeswax (which gives them a subtle scent of honey, too), so after a label is sewn to the bottle it serves as a drip guard as well as a label. Our biggest challenges have been sourcing the raw materials and specialized tools. We end up making a lot of our own tools—our double screenprinter, for example," says Gilbert.

STUDIO BOOT

Studio Boot is a two-person design studio in the Netherlands made up of Petra Janssen and Edwin Vollebergh. For the project shown here, Studio Boot teamed up with Sister Priscilla of the Foundation of the Holy Cross and with the Dutch Foundation Home Plan to create the packaging for No House Wine. The profits of this product are used to build homes for the orphaned children of HIV/AIDS victims in South Africa. In addition to housing, the children receive food, education, and development opportunities. "The challenge was to create a label for a product that supports a good cause without referring to pitiful children or sick people. We didn't want buyers to associate with all the sadness. We wanted to create an appealing, distinct look," says Vollebergh.

The No House Wine packaging is based on ultra-low-cost production and use of pre-existing packaging materials, such as the silver bubble envelopes, cardboard packaging material, and netting. "We went through several packaging manufacturers' catalogs to pick out the items we could use," explains Vollebergh. "The design for the labels consists mainly of handmade type in a way that refers to labeling of bottles by producers during the process of wine making. This is simple, direct,

and personal: good wine in good, simple packaging." The labels are applied by hand, resulting in every bottle being slightly different. Studio Boot employs a silkscreen technique that prints glass enamel ink directly onto bottles. Their hand-drawn illustrations and type provide a beautiful, personal, and cost-effective design solution for this product. Custom-printed tape is also a cost-effective and functional option for adding a bit of informative flair to the silkscreened bottles.

1-2. Client: No House Wine
Hand-drawn illustrations and type, hand-assembled.

ATIPUS DESIGN

Atipus is a design studio established in Barcelona in 1998. For their organic, handmade product 1270 A Vuit Wine, the client, Celler Hidalgo Albert, a family-run winery in Spain, wanted the label to reflect the character of the wine and the traditional process that is a result of the family effort.

To create the label and identity of the wines, Atipus wanted to simulate a manual label-making process, without using a computer. To reflect the handmade nature of the wine, the design for the label was based on hand-stamping and is meant to convey the idea of family members making the labels themselves. The label was printed industrially, but its design process was completed using hands-on methods. The title characters are prints of cut-outs of type and numbers on cardboard. Due to the limited resources, and to highlight the handmade characteristics, the label contains just two colors.

1. Client: Celler Hidalgo Albert
Hand-generated type and numbers.

In November of each year, coinciding with the traditional Catalan celebration of the slaughtering of the pig, Vi Novell is bottled. This fruity wine is bottled before its fermentation is finished and, therefore, doesn't mature in the bottle, so must be consumed within a short space of time.

Atipus' design for this product recalls the look of a poster printed with traditional wood type. "Our aim was to create a label that could serve as a poster to announce the party as well as the wine. For this, we created the type of graphic you would get by using wood type, characterized by the imperfections of the print and the boldness of the broad type," says partner Eduard Duch. "We drew inspiration from the typical poster put up for town parties, made out of large pieces of wood, so as to be made quickly and seen well."

2. Client: Celler el Masroig
Hand-drawn illustrations and type.

MASH DESIGN

Mash Design is an Australian branding agency that has created some incredibly memorable and beautiful work since 2002, the year it was founded by Dom Roberts and James Brown.

Mash has created a full body of work across a lot of media, but they shine in particular when creating labels and bottles for wine companies. Here is a very small selection of work they've created that has a handmade touch or feel.

Mash was approached by Justin Lane, a wine evangelist who, after years of making other people's wines famous, wanted to collaborate to create a unique brand. The trick was to figure out how to put years of stories, old-school methods, made-up methods, and other personal history onto a wine label. "We realized the brand name and the world's first alphabet of wines in Justin's tin shed, which is now known as The AB&D [Alpha Box & Dice—see image 1] Wine Salon. This was given the Mash hand-painted touch. Each wine is unique, but like a film project, the 26 letters have 26 stories that are all interconnected."

For another project, Mash needed to come up with a package that could hold a selection of Evo products to be used by sales reps when visiting potential and existing buyers. Mash's solution was to source a variety of used vintage cases. They then screenprinted the outsides of the cases and customized the insides with pink satin to hold each Evo product (see image 2).

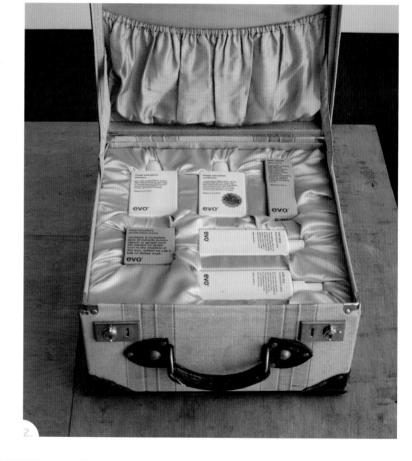

 1. Client: Alpha Box & Dice
Hand-painted type and designs.

 2. Client: EVO
Screenprinting and upcycling.

Sarah and Sparky Marquis of Mollydooker approached Mash to create a new brand for their wines. Because of its attention to detail and hands-on approach, Mash decided to design the packaging without any computer-generated fonts—all type was hand-drawn.

Inspiration came from antique books and old advertising illustrations. Working with John Englehardt, Mash created their own illustrations based on the names of the wines. With the rolling out of these labels, Mollydooker brand awareness shot through the roof.

3. Client: Mollydooker
Hand-drawn type.

The founders of boutique winery Linnaea both have backgrounds in medical anthropology and plant biochemistry, so it is unsurprising that they named their wines using the Linnaean binomial system of nomenclature. Linnaea Rhizotomi (see image 1) was the first release.

Rhizotomists, the forefathers of medics and chemists, had knowledge of plant roots and their medicinal effects. Following research into botanical images and working through a variety of collages to build a handmade aesthetic, Mash created a modern-day, slightly twisted, and beautiful interpretation of a rhizotomist, resulting in a unique and surreal package.

Another of Mash's wine clients, Magpie Estate, have a super-premium product (see image 2), which they wanted to sit apart from the other wines in their range. While the logo remains consistent as a secondary element, the bottle design and printing methods depart from the other Magpie Estate wines. A beautiful imported French bottle was chosen, and the bird illustration and text details were screenprinted directly onto the bottle. No paper labels were used—even the back label details are screenprinted.

1.

 1. Client: Linnaea Winery
Handmade aesthetic.

At the top end of Redheads' fine wines is the product Return of the Living Red (see image 3). This nonvintage wine has no age (the two grape varieties come from different vintages). To complement this fact, Mash developed a concept to create a small pack containing missing and/or suppressed crime files, implying the existence of the living dead in and around the vineyards. The concept was brought to life through the use of disturbing illustrations and fascinating old photos on a toothy, uncoated paper. A slipknot tied in old twine and a blood-red, wax-dipped bottle went with the old crime-file folder to create what Mash says is one of their favorite pieces. "We had to employ someone to tie the noose to each bottle by hand. Not only this, but they also had to dip each bottle in the blood-red wax to seal the top. The cards and envelope were sheet-fed for printing and assembled by hand," says Brown.

2. Client: Magpie Estate
Hand-drawn illustration, screenprinting.

3. Client: Redheads Wine Studio
Hand-drawn illustration, hand-finishing.

SMITH & MILTON

Smith & Milton opened its doors for business in Battersea, London, UK, in 1980. Now, just over 30 years later, it is recognized as one of the UK's leading brand identity design companies. These brand experts work with some of the most successful businesses in the UK and beyond. Their team questions, shapes, and aims to develop brands that will be even more relevant and valuable tomorrow than they are today.

Percy & Reed's "hair." is a range of styling and hair-care products developed and originated by celebrity hairdressers Adam Reed and Paul Percival. Smith & Milton were tasked with developing a brand and range of packaging that reflects British individuality, lifestyle, and personality. Smith & Milton designer Caroline Phillips

created a bespoke fashion illustration (see image 1) for each of the uniquely named products. The girl in each illustration is inspired by a British fashion icon to evoke quintessentially eccentric British style and, of course, fabulous hair.

"In a product environment that already contains so much color and busyness, we explored a more premium feel for Percy & Reed's 'hair.' range of shampoos, conditioners, and other essential hair-care products," says Brand Manager Rosie Milton. "We kept the style simple: black for the text, pencil graphite for the illustrations (straight from Caroline Phillip's sketchbook pages onto the pack) on a light cream, and let the Percy & Reed 'girls' do the talking. Acting as spokeswomen for each of the products, they are accompanied by their

own playful, idiosyncratic phrase that refers to the product's utility: 'In a hurry? Don't get yourself into a lather!' for No-Fuss Fabulousness Dry Shampoo, or 'Does my hair look big in this?' for Bountifully Bouncy Volumising Conditioner, for instance."

The use of classic, more masculine typefaces sets off the very feminine illustrations and the softer, hand-drawn statements that appear on each pack. The use of monochrome further promotes a sense of stylish vintage, influenced by gentrified Victorian England—a strong theme in the Percy & Reed brand.

1.

1–3. Client: Percy & Reed
Hand-drawn illustrations.

2.

3.

HEATHER NGUYEN

Heather Nguyen is a freelance graphic designer based in Vancouver, British Columbia, Canada. "In my work I believe that simplicity is an art and that intention is the sole root of all results. My area of design interest is typography and branding. I'm happiest when I can combine these two design interests to create a memorable and loved brand."

For this project the client, Mikuni Wild Harvest, asked Nguyen to work on the branding for their product line Noble Handcrafted, a brand that embraces the collaboration of craft with the pioneering of the new American food tradition. Each design element of this brand, from its name to the typography, is inspired

from the period of Prohibition, or "The Noble Experiment." Each design element was chosen to meet the vision of creating a brand that matched its contents—exclusively handcrafted.

Nguyen conducted research into the Prohibition era. "During this time, most liquor was underground so that meant printing on old beautiful letterpresses with wood or metal letters. This brought on the inspiration that the label needed to feel aged or from a letterpress," she says.

She created image files from rolling ink on paper to create the texture and layered it onto the typography. To make the labels

feel aged, they printed on an uncoated, fibrous, off-white stock with a special black ink combination that helps to create depth. The typography is inspired by letterpress and the choppy, masculine fonts used during the time of the Prohibition. Each label is designed to match the needs of each product content and bottle size, but still retain the spirit of the Noble Handcrafted brand.

The product line consists of five products packaged in apothecary-inspired bottles. A cork stopper mirrors the handcrafted feel, finished off by a cream-colored wax that is dipped and spun by hand. The client went through a few trials to get the wax to dip just right.

1.

 1-3. Client: Mikuni Wild Harvest
Hand-made textures, letterpress printing, hand-applied labels, hand-dipped wax.

2.

3.

MILLER CREATIVE

New Jersey (USA)-based Miller Creative is a full-service branding and packaging design agency with a wealth of experience in gourmet food, health, beauty products, and more.

"Our approach to packaging always begins with asking a few questions: 'Who are we selling to? Who are we competing with? How is this product different/better?'" says principal Yael Miller. "Once we can answer those questions, we look at the brand's personality (or create one from scratch!) and allow that to influence the entire brand experience, and most importantly the packaging, on every level. The more consistently we can do it, the better. With The Painted Pretzel, we wanted to take the brand away from a typical mom-and-pop feel and move it toward a gourmet, boutique feel that was classic and modern all at once. We think we achieved this through combining a traditional and symmetrical design approach, letterpress printing, and bright, non-traditional color combinations.

"Letterpress printing really makes the packaging irresistible. The genuine, tactile feel of this printing process cannot be matched by any other. When you print letterpress, it's more cost-effective to group elements on a sheet and to maximize what you can get in the layout. We were able to fit more on the sheets than just the labels and we decided to print little side-seals for the packaging instead of using vinyl seals. They added a wonderful handcrafted element to the finished package."

1.

2.

1-4. Client: Painted Pretzel LLC
Hand-drawn illustration, letterpress printing, hand-applied seals.

3.

4.

Miller describes the challenges his company faced with this project. "The containers were made by two vendors: one supplied the plastic tubes and the other made the caps. We also designed the packaging to fit two products by making the labels fit the same diameter, but on containers of different heights. This way, the plastics supplier could keep costs down for us."

"With printing, the registration was very tight and setting up the separations for each plate was very complicated. Studio on Fire [a letterpress printing studio] was able to achieve a very high-quality finished product. We also had to print the pretzel illustration (which contains a hidden 'double P') out of one ink color, so getting the halftone level just right was challenging (and we still had no idea how dark or light it would turn out until we got the final prints!)."

LABELS GALLERY

Aesthetic Apparatus
Client: Andrews and Dunham Damn Fine Tea
Each label is screenprinted by hand in the
Aesthetic Apparatus studio. They use ink that is
thicker than offset-printing ink, resulting in very
rich colors. A limited quantity of each
series of tea and labels is produced to
keep things fresh.

Peter Gregson Studio
Client: Monastery Sopocani
All products in this line of juices are organic and
natural. Thus, the label uses hand-written type,
complementing the spirit of the product.

Tandem Design (photographer: Terence Mahone)
Client: Tandem Ciders
The design for this label series relies heavily on a color system and concise,
quick-witted copy describing each varietal. The "Dan's Damn Special Blend"
label is fun and flexible. This customizable label design enables
experimentation in Dan's fermentations. Write-in areas for the flavor,
variety, cider characteristics, and alcohol content, keep everything
flexible, yet still looking fancy.

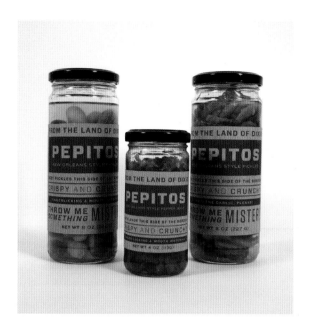

Dever Thomas
Client: Pepito's Pickles
Classic typefaces and kraft paper give these labels a traditional letterpress poster feel, but at a cheaper cost. The client prints the labels out herself on her printer at home and applies them by hand.

Duncan/Channon
Client: Farrier Wine
Designer Jennifer Moe explains the inspiration behind the design for this project. "The design tells the story of a blacksmith shop that had been on the property in the 1800s. It was a place where the local farrier (horseshoe fitter) plied his trade and the townsfolk gathered to socialize. Reinforcing the handcrafted quality of the wine, the packaging mirrors the look of an old newspaper and the language adopts an endearingly olde school colloquial tone that hearkens back to the handicraft traditions of the pre-Industrial age. We distressed the type and used a pronounced halftone dot pattern on some of the artwork to give it that printed-on-a-letterpress-in-1895 look."

Lorena Mondragón Rodríguez (photographer: Luis Jasso)
Personal project
Through inspiration from signs used by homeless people, a simple BBQ sauce bottle, a box, or a paper bag becomes a social statement that is designed to spark conversations about homelessness among families and friends while they are cooking or eating in the comfort of their homes. Rodríguez sketched the typography herself. All the elements of the design, from illustrations to typography, are rendered by hand. She used marker pens to write the text and draw the images. She then scanned everything and edited it in Photoshop. The labels were digitally printed and individually applied by her.

LABELS GALLERY

David Arias
Client: Belmondo Skin Care
Arias explains his thinking behind this label design: "I wanted the design to have a humanistic look and feel, so I decided to create a hand-rendered type form to be used as the main display face for the product. The concept was inspired by the way handmade writing is displayed on chalkboard surfaces to name and describe products at the markets. For me, black and white offers great visual contrast, while providing a classic and understated quality. I hand-rendered the type design in pencil, which was later vectorized and set on each label letter by letter. This proved to be a tedious process but also made each product more unique. By estimating the spacing between each letter on each label, the slight differences in every word would make the design more authentic—and I was drawn to that idea."

Frank Aloi
Client: Divine Dairy
"A hands-on approach was used, printing and stamping various designs and typography to achieve the distressed 'handmade' result," explains Aloi.

Gen Design Studio
Client: Confeitaria Lopes
Since Confeitaria Lopes is a small, family-owned business, the designers at Gen Design Studio decided the most effective solution for this packaging would be to use pre-made jars and tin cans, choosing components that are simple and cost-effective, but also distinctive in shape. They then designed a set of self-adhesive labels and tags inspired by the ornament and patterns on the famous Portuguese tile, as well as Portuguese soap packaging. A space is reserved on the label for the producer to write on the use-by date for each product, and the labels and tags are applied by hand. The traditional soap packaging is an interesting source of inspiration. "It's not only the perfume of old times and the quality of the handmade products, it's the marvellous patterns of the wrapping paper that make the strong visual reference, and this is exactly what inspired us," says Creative Director Leandro Veloso. "Those wrapping papers have the colors, patterns, and beauty of old times and, at the same time, the fact that they are packed with care by hand reminds us of the long tradition and proves quality."

Freshthrills
Self-promotion

For this self-promotional holiday project, each bottle of chocolate lager was labeled by hand with labels letterpress-printed by The Cranky Pressman, and packaged into a wooden box bearing a rubber stamp of the Motorman branding. The designers then digitally printed personalized hang-tags and hand-applied a wood-textured paper backing for each recipient. A set of four unique coasters was also packaged, bound by a hand-cut and hand-folded bellyband.

Mads Jakob Poulson
Client: Ribe Bryghus Brewery

For this beer-packaging project, Poulson was inspired by old sign painting and hand-carved letters. He wanted the design of the label to feel crafted and almost handmade —just like the beer it is labeling. Poulson created a custom typeface inspired by old signage typography on the computer. The typeface was then printed out and he redrew the whole thing by hand with a fountain pen to add to the hand-crafted texture of the packaging. He then finalized the typeface on the computer and it became the basis for the packaging design and logo of Ribe Bryghus Brewery.

Depot WPF
Personal project

This packaging project focuses on black-and-white graphic patterns of things found in the environment of a small dairy farm, which reflect the naturalness of dairy production and of the products themselves. The objective was to make the product stand out on the store shelf and distinguish it from the products of other dairy producers. The illustrations were hand-drawn with a pencil, then scanned in.

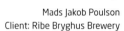

CHAPTER 6 TAGS

This chapter focuses on some tags that serve a much higher purpose than just denoting price. These tags are an integral part of the design of the packaging and, in many cases, elevate it into a piece that has the distinct mark of being crafted by hand. These tags are not the type you rip off with frustration—they're arguably keepsakes.

CHEN DESIGN ASSOCIATES

Chen Design Associates has been producing high-quality design work for almost 20 years. "Our work is guided by ambitious design thinking and is grounded in the particular needs of each client," says Principal Josh Chen. "We are streamlined to stay nimble and personal even as our projects increase in size and scope. Because we are experts, not egoists, we engage clients in the process to foster respect and fuel invention."

CDA collaborated with chef William Werner to develop the branding and packaging for his venture, Tell Tale Preserve Co., which offers traditional bakery items with a modern twist by incorporating seasonal flavors and local ingredients.

"We didn't start out with the goal of creating handmade packaging for his products but, given the inevitable challenges that come with birthing a new brand in a tough economy with limited funds, that was exactly what was needed," says Chen.

Inspiration was drawn from antique packaging pieces. "But we also didn't want to get stuck with something that was just drawn from antique packaging; we wanted to mix that up with Chef's personality, his outlook, his approach, his way of doing things a little bit unexpected with a little rock and roll," says Chen. "Baked goods tend to be presented as female, pink, and pretty, so we wanted to avoid that. Chef Werner sourced the pre-stained tags, which were then letter-pressed. The date is stamped on with custom rubber stamps that CDA designed for each month. Typography is used in unexpected ways. The graphics and illustrations are a little bit wacky and offbeat and the materials that we used have a handmade vernacular with unexpected extras like foil stamping or brass eyelets on top of a tag wrapped around a burlap bag. I think that reflects his whole approach, which is about combining unexpected ingredients together."

1.

1-2. Client: Tell Tale Preserve Company
Letterpress printing, hand stamping, hand finishing.

SOMETHING'S HIDING IN HERE

Stephen Loidolt and Shauna Alterio of Something's Hiding in Here (see also page 150) make all of their products by hand. "Small tokens of affection are our obsession. Most of our products start life as a small gift we make for each other or friends. We were both educated in a 'form follows function' academic setting, and this method of creating is at the core of our aesthetic," says Shauna. Shauna and Stephen create their packaging and tags by hand, usually employing the help of their letterpress.

"When we first decided to make bow ties, we were so excited that we finally had a reason to buy lots and lots of vintage-style mason boxes; we've been in love with them forever. Everything else fell into place. Our logo and printing is a direct result of the vintage letterpress type we had on hand. We also silkscreened the printing on the boxes," explains Shauna.

"We rely on techniques that we are familiar with and tools that we have on hand. Letterpress and silkscreen are at the top of our go-to list. We love simple and inexpensive materials—kraft tag board is another favorite that we love to work with."

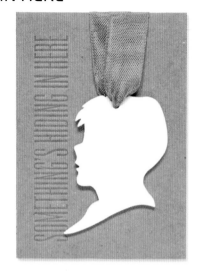
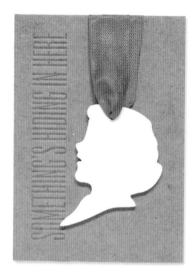

1-2. Personal project
Letterpress printing, hand finishing.

3-5. Personal project
Silkscreening, hand finishing.

LEONARDO DI RENZO

Leonardo Di Renzo is a graphic designer based in Italy. Before becoming a designer, he attended schools related to agriculture, but was driven by his love for art and design to pursue graphic design at the Istituto Europeo di Design in Rome. From there, he worked as a screen designer, then at a printing press, followed by a packaging company, and finally as a graphic designer with various studios and advertising agencies. After designing labels and packaging for hundreds of clients, Di Renzo decided he should design something for himself. Thus, TYPUGLIA (Puglia—a region in Italy—plus typography) was born out of his two passions: printing and his land.

Di Renzo's first product offering is an eco-friendly, recyclable kit that includes a handmade, hand-colored earthenware bottle containing extra virgin olive oil from Southern Italy, a hand-printed tag, a reusable box (which can be repurposed into a lamp, as shown in image 4), original wooden type blocks, and a small bag of olive leaves from the tree the olive oil originated from.

Di Renzo says, "The tags are made completely by hand, and are manually printed with a printing press roller. The inspiration for the tags arose after seeing vintage packaging in movies from the fifties."

1.

1–4. Personal project
Hand printing, hand finishing.

2.

3.

4.

PERKY BROS

Perky Bros, a graphic design studio located in Nashville, Tennessee, USA, is run by Jefferson Perky. It specializes in identity, print, web, and package design, and strives to "speak plainly and be honest ..."

For the design of the shirt hangtags shown in images 1, 2, and 3 for Red Kap, a provider of workwear uniforms, the goal was to create a no-nonsense tag for a no-nonsense product, and to strike a balance between a limited-edition gift and utility. The cards were completed by hand and the limited-edition gifts were then sent to Red Kap's top 300 distributors.

Perky created a complete package for his set of guitar strings, shown on the opposite page, including a how-to-get-started guide. The materials and lettering used give the set a wonderful tactile quality. The package, wallets, and disc were screenprinted.

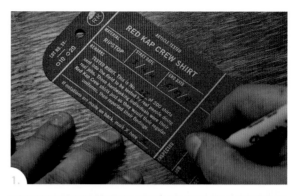

1.

2.

3.

1–3. Client: Red Kap
Handwriting.

For another client, Perky Bros designed a tag that doubles as a business card for the client, Hazel and Delt. "Specializing in repurposed and handmade merchandise, this boutique needed a card and tag that stayed true to its principles. The solution was a budget-friendly business card that doubles as a tag. These were letterpress-printed on chipboard. By combining the tag and the business card and limiting the design to one color, we were able to produce these with higher quality. Each card is turned into a tag by filling out the forms by hand," explains Perky.

4.

5.

4. Personal project
Screenprinting.

5. Client: Hazel and Delt
Letterpress printing.

YUJO! CREATIVIDAD APLICADA

YuJo! Creatividad Aplicada is a design studio based in Mexico that was founded in 2009 with a focus on advertising. YuJo! soon realized their clients were dealing primarily with branding issues, so shifted their focus to naming and packaging.

"When we were first presented to Creencias Organic Tequila, we instantly knew we had a great product at its core. But the way it looked was just not working for anyone," says partner Joel Gutiérrez. "Here was an all-organic product, with a Saverglass French bottle that degrades in only three years, and we needed to create a label. We wanted to remain true to the natural spirit of the product, so we chose not to use any adhesives. After some thought, we decided on a hang tag, which was great because no other tequila that we knew of was using anything similar. The tag is printed on Bristol board but has a jute tag underneath screenprinted with black ink. Then came the idea for the natural henequén that winds around the bottlenecks and connects to the tag. This string is handmade in Yucatán, México by just a few families. We loved the idea of a clean design that, unlike most, lets you see the whole product. We also liked the possibility of people removing the string and the tag after they're done, then reusing the bottle for any other purpose."

The look and feel of the tag were inspired by the traditional hacienda lifestyle. Before the designers formally began working on the project, they visited Hacienda Santa Cruz del Valle, where a *troje* was still on its feet. The troje is the place where, traditionally, the hacienda's grains were stored, and also where the hacienda workers came, week after week, for their salary. The designers wanted to share the feeling of a product made by the workers for the workers.

"The most difficult decision for the client to make was to have handmade packaging for a mass-production tequila. Although Creencias is not such a big name, they did start out with 40,000 bottles that were all hand-labeled. This was great because even though it was slow and expensive, each bottle was unique," says Gutierrez.

 1–4. Client: Creencias Tequila Orgánico
Screenprinting, string and tag applied by hand.

PEG AND AWL

Peg and Awl was created in January of 2010 by Margaux and Walter Kent a few months after Walter returned to Philadelphia from serving in Iraq. Margaux had been making books and jewelry. Walter had been working with his father as a cabinet-maker until he left for Iraq. The couple wanted to start something together, but were not sure what it would be. Eventually, they began to fabricate home goods such as their candle blocks, caddies, and totes from "old things, treasures found and recovered from misfortune and neglect, relics of the unusual, the confused, and the macabre, cut and pulled and bound into wearable curiosities, inscribable keepsakes, and usable treasures...
Peg and Awl has been evolving since the very beginning and I do so hope it doesn't stop!" explains Margaux.

She continues, "As for packaging, no detail is skipped over. Walter had some dreadful stories, not of war, but of the painful process of identification that comes with being in the military. Everything has a number, a description, a count, a routine, a process—oftentimes just for the sake of order. I saw a crumpled-up military tag—for luggage or something—somewhere and thought it would be a good starting point for us. After all, each one of the objects we make not only has a present purpose, it had a past, a history entirely different to what it has become. We thought we needed to tell the story. At first we had oversized tags, just like those in the military, that we printed ourselves. They were bulky and kind of icky and wasteful, so we made them smaller. And smaller. And smaller."

Margaux continues, "We met another husband-and-wife team at a craft show. They have a letterpress studio. I didn't know when, but I knew we wanted to work with them. It took a little organization, learning how to use computers, and creating a logo, to commit. The tags went even smaller. And letterpressed, they were perfect! We began to create different tags for different products, each with spaces to fill in the details." The resulting hand-printed tags, labels (made from unique decoupaged pages of antique books circa 1880), and hand-finished packaging have a rustic, simple feel that reinforces the ethos behind the making of their hand-crafted products.

 1–3. Personal project
Letterpress printing, decoupage, handwriting

"Our packaging includes a lot of little details," says Margaux, "so we wanted to try to simplify things so as to not have too many tags—this was/is a challenge. Another challenge is working with companies (like Anthropologie) who require us to put their barcodes on our tags. We have to create packaging to fit those—so in some instances we wrap our product with brown paper and stamp Peg and Awl onto it."

TAGS GALLERY

Kristen Magee
Personal project

Designer Kristen Magee wanted these canning tags to have a worn, vintage feel, so she initially drew rough sketches of canning jars in different sizes and shapes using pencil and paper. She then scanned the sketches and digitized them in Adobe Illustrator.

Josh Gordon Creative
Personal project

A simple tag can have a big impact. These tags for bundles of handmade cards were created from unwanted, unused shipping tags and stamped by hand with a custom-made stamp.

Jessica Packard
Personal project

Linen-finish paper and hand stitching (visible on the round tags) give these herb kits a warm, friendly feel.

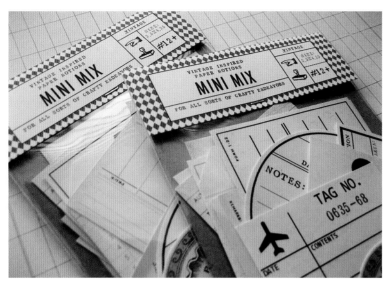

France Wisniewski
Client: Bananafishstudio
A combination of clean design, recycled paper, and a handcrafted letterpress feel is an apt hallmark of Wisniewski's packaging for these vintage-style paper products and supplies.

Stitch Design Co.
Client: Low Country Local First
These invitations, printed with three colors on a letterpress printer, were die-cut and attached to a burlap bag with a custom-wrapped fabric button. The empty burlap bag was folded down and mailed, with the tag serving as the invitation itself. The fabric buttons attached the tag to the bag. The recipient of the invitation could easily remove the tag and button and then keep the bag to use.

Eric Kass at Funnel
Client: Abigail Mayfield
"Abigail Mayfield is an artist with a love of unconventional, rough, raw beauty. She also has an important family connection to antiques and heirlooms, which inform her work," explains Kass. "I created a distressed design letterpress-printed on chipboard to be used as business cards and tags (inspired by antique paint tubes, that have room for writing painting details,) and a hand-applied grommet so that Abigail can add her own bits of found items that relate to her work. These tags are attached to the back of the paintings and tied with twine to the outside of the brown Kraft-paper-wrapped paintings when they are delivered to patrons."

CHAPTER 7 BOXES

Ah, the humble box. It has come a long way since being first used by the Kellogg Company in the early twentieth century to package their cereals. This chapter showcases boxes that have been screenprinted, adorned with hand-applied stickers and gorgeous illustration work, letterpressed, and even assembled by hand to become something far beyond a humble old box.

ILOVEDUST

ilovedust uses a range of techniques for every project, from pen and ink sketches and screenprinting to working on a Wacom with Photoshop and Illustrator. They have mock-ups made at each stage in the development of the brand so that the designers and the client can visualize the finished work and understand the process and the direction they are moving toward. For the project shown here, they spent time getting to grips with the feel of the brand.

"Allotinabox is a mini garden kit intended to encourage people to grow their own fruit and vegetables. The mixture of slab serif and serif typefaces used within the logo comes from inspiration fueled by research into allotments and the eclectic mix of found/used items that people use to help identify their own allotments.

We used a letterpress stamp technique, which gives the box a hand-printed feel, referring to the 'hands on,' grubby aspect of growing. The brand is always evolving, with different contents for boxes with seasonal themes."

 1–2. Client: Allotinabox
Hand assembly.

HEYDAYS

Heydays is a five-person, multidisciplinary design company based in Oslo, Norway. The five set up the company in 2008 right after graduating (all from the same class) and work with conceptual and functional design for a wide range of businesses, and organizations.

They created their own packaging for use with clients. "We wanted a very functional set of stationery and packaging that could be used every day in our studio as well as for client presentations and sending out packages. It is partly inspired by warehouse packaging, partly inspired by functionality. The use of chrome material was inspired by our name and by Andy Warhol's silver factory (and silver clouds)," says designer

Lars Kjelsnes. The most challenging aspect of the project was that they were designing for themselves. Kjelsnes says, "It's a challenge in itself—often harder than working for a client. Working with our own set of restrictions and rules helped a lot."

To implement the package design they set up some ground rules: no colors were to be added—all tonal variations had to come through the materials used—and Monospace was to be the only typeface used.

Once the ground rules were established, the process flowed smoothly. The team incorporated a range of tools and techniques in the creation of the stationery kit, including screenprinting, embossing, custom die cuts, custom tape, and offset printing. The tape, custom-printed with the studio's information, allows almost any item to become a branded package. The tape allows for the boxes and other items to be instantly branded. The very plain boxes, branded with the tape, look smart yet utilitarian.

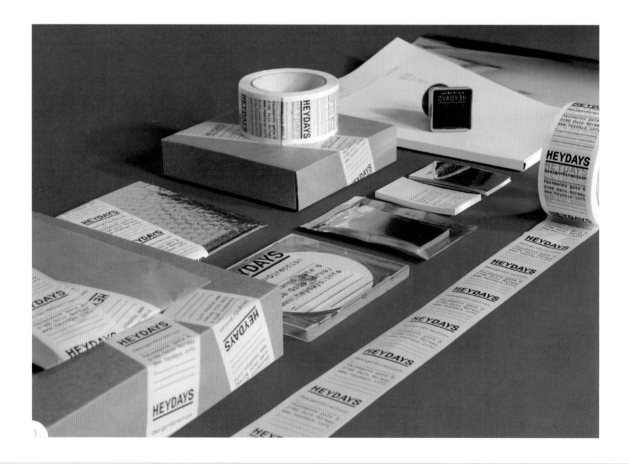

1.

1-4. Self-promotion
Screenprinting, embossing, custom die cuts, custom tape, hand finishing.

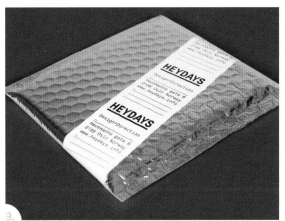

LAUREN ROGERS

Lauren Rogers graduated in 2009 after completing her Bachelor of Arts in Communication Design, specializing in Digital Design at Queensland College of Art in Brisbane, Queensland, Australia. She has since worked as a graphic designer, both freelance and in several design firms. She created this packaging concept for an academic project. "Savian Soap Co. is a natural soap range in need of a rebrand to freshen its image and raise its status within the current market," says Rogers. "Using a fresh color palette, modern typography, clean design, and thoughtful choice in packaging material, this rebranding would modernize the brand."

After researching leading soap brands, a target audience was identified, and a style and pattern were developed to create a feminine, organic feel for the brand. Fresh, bright colors were chosen to convey the nature of each product in the range, but also to convey the overall feel of the brand. The colorful inner box provids a subtle way of incorporating bright color into the package and complements the hints of color on the outside boxes. From the side you can see a strip of color, but it's not until you slide the slip off the box that the full color of the box is revealed. The functionality of having an inner box and an outer slip means the customer can easily slide the soap out to look at it without having to destroy the packaging.

Each of the boxes was cut and folded by hand. The process for creating the boxes began with the design of the dielines (Rogers created two dielines: one for the inner box and one for the outer slip), test printing, and testing the shapes by mocking up the boxes and slips until they fit perfectly. A lot of testing was done to ensure the correct stock was used

for the inner box, as this had to have enough weight to retain its shape and help to maintain the outer slip's shape, too. The chosen paper stock was thick, tactile, and toothy, which conveys the organic feeling of the brand. The paper stock allows the soap's scent to permeate, and also holds ink well.

Swing tags with information about the soap were attached to organic cotton string that was then wrapped around the boxes, creating an extra pop of color.

1.

2.

1–5. Academic work
Handmade boxes, hand assembly.

3.

4.

5.

WALLNUT

Founded in 2007, Wallnut is a graphic design, textile, and branding studio run by Colombian graphic designer Cristina Londoño. It has a reputation for generating contemporary works developed from a profound passion for color, an obsession for detail, and a lust for research, all applied to concepts, surfaces, fashion, prints, and interiors, among other things.

The high-end Marypat Pastry Shop hired Wallnut to create their pastry packaging. Inspired by vintage French suitcases that have "seen the world," Wallnut created a flexible and fun project comprising a set of stickers, stamps, and cards. Mixing these elements anew each time a pastry is packaged allows each home-delivered product to arrive in a visually fresh way while maintaining the brand's cohesive visual identity.

The packaging was developed in various sizes, allowing the company to package everything from small cookies and medium desserts to huge cakes. Londoño says the most challenging aspect of this project was coming up with a concept that could be so flexible. "Marypat was a very small company at that time. It couldn't afford big inventories of packaging material, didn't have a big budget, and was trying out many different products in its portfolio, each one varying in size and requirements. The design solution had to be very practical and easy to customize for every situation. The design process required a lot of mock-ups and trial and error but, most importantly, it became the main guideline for, and strength of, the project. Finding quick and inexpensive printing methods and allowing the client space for creativity at the moment of packaging were our best resources."

"In search of the most flexible solutions," Londoño continues, "we came up with a combination of offset- and laser-printed items in paper and card stock, combined with a set of ink stamps. The solution involves just a single, one-color printed surface design for all the boxes and, for those, we use sizes that already exist in the market. To complement the development we created a set of laser-printed stickers in easy-to-cut sizes that, combined in creative ways, would create a different look for every product."

1–4. Client: Marypat Pastry Shop
Hand finishing.

3.

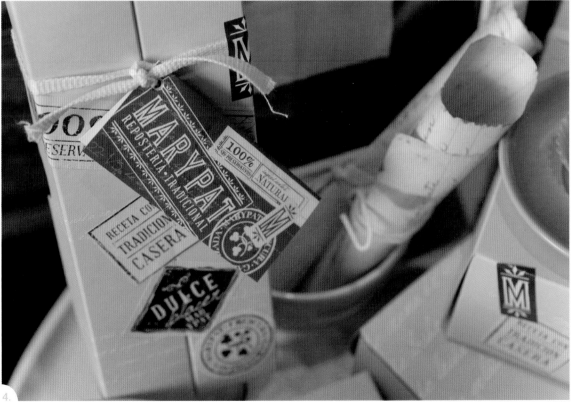

4.

AESTHETIC APPARATUS

Aesthetic Apparatus is a printmaking and graphic design studio based in Minneapolis, Minnesota, USA. The idea for the studio took seed when Dan Ibarra and Michael Byzewski first met in 1998 while working as designers. Combining their mutual interest in printmaking and music, the two began to build a groundwork of limited-edition hand-printed concert posters that gained them enough recognition nationally and internationally to convince them to "turn their measly late-night beer-fueled hobby into a full-time graphic design studio," says Ibarra. As a fully functioning studio—able to handle a full spectrum of design projects along with the posters they love so much—Aesthetic Apparatus has created work for clients such as Blue Q, Stella Artois, HarperCollins, the American Cancer Society, and Criterion Collection, as well as bands such as Cake, Frank Black, The Hold Steady, The New Pornographers, Spoon, Dinosaur Jr, Grizzly Bear, and more. Their work has been featured in a number of design books and in many magazines, including *Print*, *Step Into Design*, *Swindle*, *Communication Arts*, *Creative Review*, *HOW*, *Print*, *Rolling Stone*, *Jane Magazine*, and *Readymade Magazine*.

 1–2. Client: Two Bettys Green Cleaning Service
Screenprinting, hand assembly.

2.

Two Bettys is a Minneapolis-based green house-cleaning company that is a bit more irreverent than a typically straight-faced or pensive green company. The clients needed packaging that reflected their personalities, the name "Two Bettys," and green cleaning. The final identity is composed of elements and language that satirize explicitly non-green, mid-century American industrial-chemical visual language, the cultural vernacular of "clean," as well as the idea and the language of "green." These boxes serve as calling-card displays, the main form of communication between Two Bettys and potential clients.

Ibarra and Byzewski say that one of the most complicated aspects of creating this packaging was that the box required a long series of variations and experiments to determine the final dieline. This glueless dieline is designed to emulate detergent boxes. The boxes were produced in-house at Aesthetic Apparatus (along with the business cards) as a set of three-color screenprinted boxes that were then trimmed by a local die cutter and assembled by the client as needed.

ZOO STUDIO

Zoo Studio is a graphic and multimedia agency located in Spain. Rubén Álvarez is a chocolate artist with whom Zoo Studio has worked closely on several projects. Two of them are featured here.

Zoo Studio created the packaging for a limited-edition chocolate artwork entitled Code Egg (see image 1.) The packaging contains a chocolate egg that copies a real egg in its color, texture, and shelf life. The product is made of dark chocolate and painted with cocoa butter with white food coloring. The label is an adhesive paper designed to look like a typical receipt. The laser-cut carton was used together with the adhesive label to give the product a daily and domestic look, and each hand-applied label is individually signed by the artist, giving the packaging its simple, handcrafted feel.

Yoghurt is one of those products of which infinite varieties have been made, seemingly leaving no room for innovation. Rubén Álvarez aimed to challenge the limitations imposed by conventional industry by creating a new range of yoghurts (see images 2 and 3). The inspiration for this range comes from the glass container often seen in supermarkets. On the bottom there's a visible layer of semi-jam made of raspberry, pineapple, apricot, or cherry, which is topped by a layer of white chocolate and yoghurt mousse, and finished with a layer of crumble.

1.

1–3. Client: Rubén Álvarez
Handwriting, hand-finishing.

The designers felt the design for the packaging had to be of high quality as well as "a breath of fresh air," using materials and techniques unused in the rest of the market. "The combination of cardboard and sealing wax suggests simplicity and sophistication within a product that is for mass consumption," says designer Sandra Fernández.

The yoghurt is presented in a cylindrical pack made of rigid cardboard lined with metallic paper (both of which are resistant to humidity). The cylinder is sealed with white sealing wax to maintain freshness inside. There is a string attached to the top part which, when pulled, breaks the wax seal to open the packaging. The color of the string subtly indicates the flavor contained inside. A sticker with the name of the flavor holds the string to the packaging. On the metallic seal at the top there is only a list of ingredients, sell-by date, and the signature of the maker. The range consists of four packs, each distinguished by the color of the string and the lettering on the sticker.

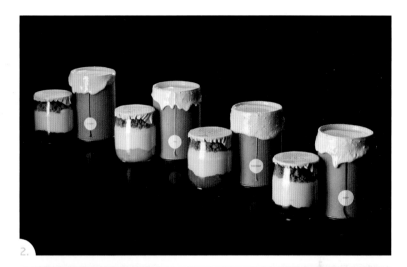

LITTLE & COMPANY

Little & Company is a firm based in Minneapolis, Minnesota, USA that's been in operation since 1979. "For design to achieve business goals, it must matter to those who encounter it. It's more than aesthetic. When design matters, it provides utility and impacts communities. It solves problems while expanding the boundaries of the craft. Our goal is to do fun, creative work that makes people smile when they think about Little & Company. And maybe spread a little love," says Design Director Ian Davies.

He continues, "Each year, we forgo the paper blizzard of holiday greeting cards to send our friends, families, and clients a Valentine mailer. Originally a marketing

tool to keep us top of mind, it has become a meaningful tradition sealed with heartfelt well wishes. There were many reasons we wanted to incorporate the aesthetics of handmade. Because the recipients are so special to us, we wanted this piece to reflect our passion, craft, and love for design. In doing things by hand, rather than digitally, it becomes even more of a personal and authentic experience—one that people will want to cherish for a long time. Mindful of the fact that everyone at Little & Company touches this project, the collective thoughtfulness speaks volumes."

The designers took inspiration from a peer's collection of vintage matchbooks to create a series of 12 collectible matchbooks under

the theme "Fuel the Love." "We wanted the matchbooks to work as a series and visually complement each other while maintaining a distinctive feel. We also wanted the piece to have a vintage feel in both illustration and message without being too gimmicky or contrived," says Davies.

Little & Company brainstormed as a group to come up with matchbook ideas. Then, several of their designers submitted their own illustrations, giving the matchbooks a distinctively eclectic feel. Every design features an illustration and expression of fiery passion. Recipients were each sent a set of three, which Little & Company hoped would inspire sharing, comparing, and swapping.

1.

1-4. Self-promotion
Hand-drawn illustrations, hand assembly, hand finishing.

Matches are considered hazardous materials and require special packaging to mail, so Little & Company had to work closely with the post office. They solved the issue by using a box-within-a-box to make sure the matchbooks could ship safely. "While we had boxes and labels printed, we had to apply each label individually to the matchboxes. Over the course of a few days, we had assembly parties and anyone who was available would come to help. The imperfections and inconsistencies of doing things by hand are just part of the charm," says Davies.

BOXES GALLERY

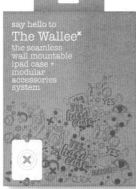

Denise Franke
Client: The Wallee

"The idea was to create a simple and charming packaging concept for The Wallee's whole range of iPad accessories that illustrates the playful, efficient, and easy-to-use character of their products. A thick cardboard was chosen for the different boxes and finished with screenprinted typography and hand-drawn illustrations to reduce the use of plastic materials," explains Franke.

Zoo Studio
Client: Cinc Sentits

The use of cardboard with a toasted brown color and a garnet-colored rope evokes the base ingredients of this product—coffee and chocolate. The pack does not envelop every corner of the product, as the designers wanted the end consumer to see the final product and admire it from the first moment. A rope holds the jar in place. The metal pieces allow the cord on the hand-assembled package to be fully tightened to ensure stability.

ilovedust
Client: Sea Cider

ilovedust was commissioned to create packaging for a cider company based in Dorset, UK. Sea Cider's packaging takes inspiration from all things maritime and features hand-drawn illustrations. Anchors and pirates mix with portholes, crabs, and shrimps to create an all-over nautical narrative in this appealing design.

Peter Gregson Studio
Client: The Manual Co.

"The Manual Co. produces everything manually and the idea behind this concept was to create packaging in the same spirit. Everything on these pieces was drawn by hand," says Gregson.

ilovedust
Client: Amelie and Friends

The branding and packaging of these take-away boxes for the restaurant Amelie and Friends (which cooks locally sourced food) was inspired by French-style bistro typefaces and has a letterpress feel. The simple, clean branding reflects the freshness of the food, the ethos, originality, and personality of the restaurant.

Owen & Stork
Client: Portland General Store

"The idea behind the grooming kit was to make something that would not only be timeless, but also get better with age. I wanted to use substantial materials—things you wouldn't be able to bring yourself to discard. The package needed to transport and deliver the grooming supplies, but it also had to become apart of the product itself. Everything was designed specifically for the kit, including individual items and labeling. All production was completed in-house at Owen & Stork. Beside the basic cutting of materials, some of the other processes used in this project were; bead blasting (logo on glass,) woodturning (shave brush and bowl,) and masking for stained graphics," says Creative Director Nicholas Wilson.

BOXES GALLERY

Nadia Arioui Salinas
Personal project
Salinas wanted this packaging to be sustainable and have a hand-crafted feel. She achieved this using biodegradable and reusable packages and hand-painted illustrations.

Popular
Client: Sofi Soaps
For this project, the designers utilized hand-written type and hand-drawn illustrations that were scanned in and printed. "On the handwritten packaging we emphasized the benefits and the ingredients of Sofi soaps, while on the illustrated packaging we tried to show the atmosphere and vibe surrounding the final usage of products," says designer Bratislav Milenkovic.

Atolón de Mororoa
Client: Librito de Mí
Librito de Mí creates personalized children's books. Low-cost packaging was needed, so the designers decided the design required an artisanal, hand-crafted solution, not only to lower production costs but also to convey the warmth and originality of the product. They sourced prefab pizza boxes and used stickers of their own design to decorate the boxes.

Camille Deann
Self-promotion

Deann is a graphic designer-turned-photographer. She uses custom stamps and sources a variety of prefab materials, from boxes to bags, to create packaging that is personal and romantic and has a vintage flair. "I wanted my packaging to be an extension of my brand, a beautiful presentation that adds to my clients' experience when they work with me," she says. "Whether it's a brochure, print, or product order, I want my clients to feel as if they're receiving a gift. My goal is to evoke exquisiteness, charm, and luxury."

Mind Design
Client: What On Earth

"What On Earth produces organic food. The packaging for their cake range was intended to be the first one in a series. In connection with the product we wanted to use illustrations with a strong handmade feel. The decision to work with lino cuts was influenced by the existing logo, which resembles the look produced by this technique. In order to design future packaging more easily, we used all illustrations on a plain background without overlaps. This way images can easily be arranged in different ways," says designer Holger Jacobs.

Devers Ink & Lead
(photographer: David Register)
Client: batch ice cream

"batch is an artisan ice-cream company that provides an alternative to products made with ingredients you can't even pronounce. The packaging design was intended to reflect the freshness and hand-crafted qualities that the batch brand stands for," says designer Wade Devers. "Drawing influence from chalkboard menus found in small city-neighborhood restaurants, we were able to reflect the essence of the brand and product. The artwork on the labels was all drawn by hand. Ice cream is a fun food and we wanted to ensure that was always reflected in the language that we used, but also in small but surprising details. For example, each package has a 'tiny landscape' unique to that flavor."

BOXES GALLERY

Rockit Science Agency
Client: Devil's Weed Cigars

"The cigars were packaged in a handmade cedar box in the Dominican Republic with a handmade brand and lettering pressed into the wood to give the authentic feel of a box from the 1500s. The packaging goal was to represent the rich history of tobacco as well as the mythology aligned with old-world cultural inspirations. The cedar boxes doubled as packaging and point-of-sale display units. Inside each box are custom illustrations that feature the history of tobacco and the introduction of tobacco to settlers," says Creative Director Joshua Dickerhoof.

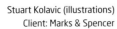

Stuart Kolavic (illustrations)
Client: Marks & Spencer

"Everything I do is hand-drawn using ink, brushes, and paper, then scanned in and colored using Photoshop," says Kolakovic. "My rough sketches are usually quite finished. I think this is because my work relies very heavily on color as opposed to line, so I find it very important to convey this to the client right from the start."

Chelsea Hendrickson
Academic project

Hendrickson created almost everything for this project by hand, from the packaging design, production, and assembly, all the way down to the making of the mustache wax itself. The box was printed on pearlescent paper using the professional printers in the Design Department at Point Loma Nazarene University, San Diego, California, USA. The mustache window was hand-cut and filled with transparency paper.

Bethany Wuerch
Personal project
Wuerch wanted to create something extra-special for her future bridesmaids. To create her bridesmaids' kits, she painted unfinished cigar boxes and lined them with vintage handkerchiefs, then added the informational cards. "In a perfect world, the lettering would have been hand-painted, but an artist has to know her limits! My painting would never have achieved the calligraphic look I desired, and so I opted for raised adhesive lettering instead."

Samantha Schneider and David Mikush
(photograper: Whitney Ott)
Academic work
Schneider and Mikush used xylene and INT transfers to place the logo onto the honey bottles, candy tins, spread jars, crates, and taster boxes. (Xylene transfers are made with black-and-white photocopies that are placed on wood or porous materials, then rubbed with a xylene marker. INTs are the logos that are on the glass—they are a smaller version of vinyl transfers used for walls and windows.) Besides the large crate, they hand-built all the boxes, labels, books, and dippers. The smaller boxes were built from basswood, balsa wood, and wood glue, then stained. The dippers were spray-painted to match the caps and tins, then glued into the caps of the honey jars.

Mind Design
(illustrator: Aude van Ryn)
Client: Le Pain Quotidien
Hand-drawn illustrations were created for this international chain and required careful collaboration between the designer and illustrator to ensure the illustrations worked well on a three-dimensional object.

CHAPTER 8 CD AND DVD CASES

CD and DVD cases combine the impact of covers, the detail of tags, and the desirability of a product in one complete package. This chapter looks at printing methods that are not typically associated with CD and DVD packaging.

ELEGANTE PRESS

Elegante Press is a small design and print studio in Lithuania with a flair for doing things differently. Saulius and Viktorija Dumbliauskien, who run the studio, love to combine hand work with work they create on their antique presses, some of which are around 100 years old. Everything that comes out of Elegante Press is handmade on their presses using 100% cotton paper and hand-mixed inks.

Kauno Grudai, a large milling company with a long history, asked Elegante Press to design a vintage-style CD package for its 120th anniversary celebration. The studio printed the CD sleeve on very heavy 500gsm paper stitched with a sewing machine and closed with a wax seal. The result, in Viktorija's words, is "pure, handmade, vintage-looking packaging." The combination of vintage-style flourishes, such as the wax seal, and letterpress printing creates a package that is tactile, luxurious, and elegant. Letterpress printing creates a palpable texture. In image 2, the lines of the clouds suggest a sense of motion that is reinforced by the deep impressions created by the press. Opening the CD sleeve reveals the letterpressed script and company logo, and the vintage scrolls on the CD itself complement the sleeve design.

1.

2.

1–4. Client: Kauno Grudai
Letterpress printing, hand-mixed inks, sewing, wax sealing by hand.

3.

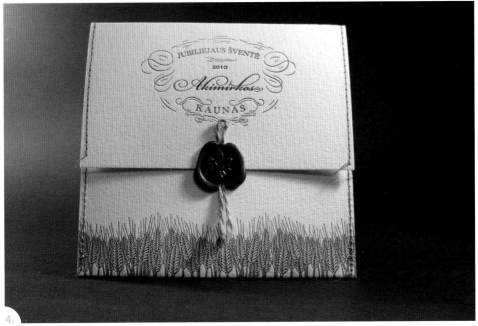

4.

MATT ELLIS

Matt Ellis is an Australian singer/songwriter who has lived in Venice, California, USA, since 2006. His music has been described as Folk Rock, Americana, and Alt-Country. Births, Deaths & Marriages, his fourth album, had a limited-edition physical release that, in addition to receiving two International Songwriting Competition awards, also became a hit with packaging and design websites and blogs. Matt, with the help of many friends, created the CD packaging himself, from start to finish.

"This album always felt a little different. I had the title early on in the writing process and kept that as an overriding theme. The songs were going a little deeper, getting more personal, and I wanted those intimate emotions and messages to translate all the way from the music through to the packaging.

"I brainstormed ideas with my wife and friends, trying to develop something that brought together everyone's three life-defining moments: birth, death, and marriage(s). The solution was a keepsake box full of items that spanned a person's life. It was something we could all relate to, yet I hadn't seen it used in music packaging before."

1.

2.

1-4. Personal project
Handwriting, hand embossing, hand stencilling.

3.

4.

"I had a tight budget, but I wanted to pack the most into these boxes. I started with the logo, presenting rough layouts and sketches to Xandra Y. Zamora, a brilliant calligrapher. Xandra helped perfect my vision, creating the logo used on both the digital cover and the boxed version. I'd always envisaged the logo embossed into a hard, linen-covered box in gold foil. The problem was how to make it look great for a small run, while keeping it affordable. After hours of searching online I found some gift boxes and ordered some to experiment with. The boxes looked great, so I started looking at ways to get the logo onto the cover. I had a 3D tool of the logo made, sprayed it with gold spray paint, and placed it and the box lids under a three-ton arbor press. With a bit of elbow grease and lots of patience, I ended up with some good-looking, hand-embossed boxes. I ordered small burlap bags to hold the CD, which I branded with a handmade stencil. I hand-wrote all the lyrics and had them reproduced on different stocks, similar to the scraps of paper I generally write on. Add to that some reproductions of photos from throughout my life and career, coins from countries I've lived in, custom Matt Ellis buttons, bottle caps from my favorite beer, gum leaves, and other flourishes, and the packs were ready to go. The finishing touch was signing each pack and numbering them all, from 1 to 500."

HAMMERPRESS

Hammerpress (see also pages 94 and 154) is a letterpress and design studio based in Kansas City, Missouri, USA. They initially developed the visual identity and collateral materials for Bearhouse, a film production studio in Kansas City. Bearhouse then tapped them to create the packaging for their showreel. Hammerpress designed and letterpressed the packaging. "While all of the other print materials stayed pretty minimal, we really wanted this piece to feel special compared to the stacks of plastic DVD cases most clients or potential clients receive," says Creative Director Brady Vest.

This piece was printed entirely on one of their Vandercook presses. The materials used were thousands of lead ornaments and border materials. "We started with a basic sketch of the layout. From there we placed all of the tiny lead pieces together on press. Once the first color was laid down, we rearranged them for the second color, and so on, until the piece was done." The resulting product has a handcrafted quality that reflects the client's dedication to quality films, and makes the product a standout among typical reel packaging.

1.

2.

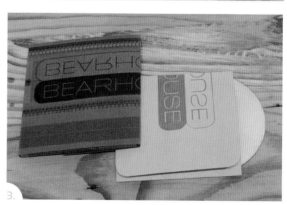

3.

1–3. Client: Bearhouse Films
Letterpress printing.

CD AND DVD CASES GALLERY

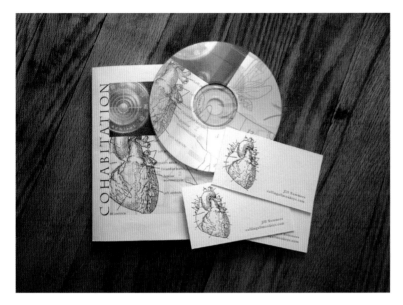

Susie Kirkwood
Client: Jill Summers

This audiobook, which Kirkwood designed in conjunction with her sister Jill Summers, uses a few different processes. The cards were letterpressed, the booklets were printed digitally, and everything was assembled by hand. The artwork is meant to provide a visual for each of the short stories on the disc. Most of them are vintage etchings of organs, butchering tools/methods, and medical diagrams. The stories give a peek into an old brownstone in Chicago and the history of its inhabitants, so a vintage feel was desirable.

Rachel Wiles
Personal project

The idea behind this packaging is love letters. Collages made of vintage imagery became postcards containing song lyrics in various handwritten typefaces. A label mimicking that of the Postal Service was affixed to a handmade box, which was finished with a button-and-string closure.

CHAPTER 9 BAGS

From illustrated coffee bags to letterpress-printed cookie-mix bags, all the bags in this chapter have a handmade touch that adds to their visual appeal. The creation processes vary but the end results all have a tactile feel to them that invites handling.

HAMMERPRESS

Hammerpress (see also pages 92 and 154) was tapped to make something that would really stand out on the shelf for the Anna Mae Southern Bread Co. after owner Shana Martin saw some other work from Hammerpress online. Her product is based on a family recipe, so Hammerpress wanted to ensure the design felt authentic and represented that heritage. The design was initially created in the press room using decades-old wood type and lead ornaments that were hand-set, one at a time, to create the layout. This design was then taken to the computer and reworked for each variation. The classic wood type and lead ornaments combined with letterpress give this packaging a unique and distinctly authentic feel.

"The bags were printed on one of our Heidelberg windmill presses. The main challenge," says Creative Director and designer Brady Vest, "was to figure out how to run these without ruining the plates due to misfeeds on press. We had to make very sure the design fell within a certain area so the printing plates would not get crushed. This was a new kind of project so we anticipated a little trial and error, but once we got that dialed in it ran pretty smoothly. The other challenge was ensuring we could do a large quantity like this, and a three-color letterpress project, efficiently and still come out ahead, moneywise. In the end, everything worked out wonderfully and Shana could not have been happier."

1.

1. Client: Anna Mae Southern Bread Co.
Letterpress printing.

FREDDY TAYLOR

Freddy Taylor is a graphic design student at Edinburgh College of Art in Scotland, UK. "I'm pretty much into everything that allows me to get into publishing, packaging, type, print, and moving image. Pushing both the concept and the boundaries of visual communication is important to my process, as I aim to combine enthusiasm with experimentation to produce strong, enjoyable final outcomes," Taylor says.

Taylor created this unique packaging concept for rebranding Geo Organics beans for an academic project. He was given simple instructions: to walk into a supermarket and pick out a brand or packet he disliked. "Beans: what can I say? Well, the current product had potential for sure; it was the first organic tinned-bean range released into supermarkets," he says. "But I was let down by the packaging. I'm aware that today's consumer wants a bit more honesty when buying organic products. With that in mind I thought I'd simply show them the beans. I tried to reflect the product's high quality by under-designing the packaging a bit and

branding them with a gentle sub-brand name: Bean Bags. This resulted in a total reinvention of the tin: a microwavable, resealable, recyclable alternative." To make this prototype, Taylor screenprinted simple,

hand-drawn type directly onto a shower curtain, then heat-sealed it with his room-mate's hair-straightening iron. The overall effect of the design gives the packaging a simple, wholesome, friendly feel.

1.

2.

1-2. Academic work
Hand-drawn type, screenprinting, hand finishing.

DESIGNBRIDGE

Farm Frites is the number-two player in the international foodservice market. In order to meet the increasing demand for food that is better for you, Farm Frites asked DesignBridge (see also page 158) to create a brand of healthier fries to challenge the product's negative perceptions.

The new sub-brand name, "Nature's Goodness," communicates the healthier brand positioning in a single-minded way. "Inspired by Farm Frites' real farm origin (their head offices are located in the original farmhouse depicted on the pack, surrounded by potato fields,) we created the ultimate natural solution—a 'potato sack' that clearly differentiates the brand, whether at point of delivery or in the freezer at the wholesalers," says Creative Director Claire Parker. Despite the bags being mass-printed, the final design evokes a feeling of naturalness, and of potato chips direct from the farm. The goal was to create a pack that caused real disruption in the category among a sea of red "fast-food" feeling products. The bag itself isn't actually burlap—the textures (see image 1) were scanned, then printed on the bags.

DesignBridge also created the packaging for the Love 2 Bake kit (see images 2–4.) Chef Julia Barclay's passion for baking was inspired during her childhood by her mother, and grew into a career that saw Julia join the production team at the TV program *Masterchef* and also work on Delia Smith's TV series *How to Cook* in the UK.

1.

2.

1. Client: Farm Frites
Handmade aesthetic.

"So often with baking, the cupboard has too much of one thing and not enough of the other. Julia's kit, Love 2 Bake, combines the finest pre-measured ingredients to make baking as simple as possible. DesignBridge was invited to create Love 2 Bake as a premium brand that expresses the simplicity and quality of the product," says Senior Designer Casey Sampson.

"We were inspired to create a design that was 'blissfully simple,' just like the ingredients. As a mirror image of the number 2 (as seen in image 4, which shows a close-up of the letterpress plate), the new heart-shaped logo links the name Love 2 Bake with the simplicity of starting with just two ingredients, and reflects the warmth of the brand's personality. Using traditional techniques, the new logo and typeface combine with hand-drawn calligraphy and are letterpressed onto uncoated paper before each pack is hand-sealed to create a beautifully crafted design." The result elevates a simple brown paper bag from something very ordinary to something with a high-end, tailored look.

2–4. Client: Love 2 Bake
Hand-drawn calligraphy, letterpress printing, hand finishing.

ABLE DESIGN

Able Design is a small design firm that's located in Philadelphia, Pennsylvania, USA. They've been around since 2008 and work with brands interested in becoming more relevant to their customers and target markets.

One Village Coffee (OVC) is a specialty roaster located outside Philadelphia. They were set up years ago with the goal of directing for-profit monetary goals to nonprofit partners in a small village in Nigeria. The CEO and start-up team had a lot of energy and quickly grew a community of followers by spending more time than the competition doing demos and tastings.

"The whole premise behind 'One Village' is to offer an open invitation to people to come together," says designer Greg Ash. "We recognize the power of the masses and, as we used to say as kids, 'two is more fun than one.'"

"We needed the bag to suggest the feel of a village. We wanted it to be entertaining, capturing conversations in different ways. We looked at a lot of visual inspiration from movements by the masses: handmade signs, petitions, and murals. Interestingly, many of the small coffee shops that serve One Village Coffee have some similar aesthetics: handwritten chalkboards, window signs, and DIY indie flyers on the bulletin board. The OVC bag needed to feel genuine and true. If it worked it might even feel like a movement." The loose handmade sketches give the packaging a casual, organic feel and, in keeping with the overall packaging concept, the typography has a handmade aesthetic.

 1–2. Client: One Village Coffee
Hand-drawn illustrations, hand-drawn typography.

TWIG & THISTLE

Kathleen Ullman is a designer based in Seattle, Washington. Twig & Thistle is a blog she started to share her personal design inspiration and DIY projects. "I design work to satisfy my own craft tooth but have also had the opportunity to craft for others. It's what I love to do and I enjoy sharing it with so many people," she says.

One of her most popular projects has been her Valentine bags (image 2). "Valentine's Day is all about those special little treats you get, so I wanted to create a simple bag that could be used for brownies or just anything sweet. I was pretty excited when I discovered that I could actually print onto flat craft bags using my inkjet printer at home. I ended up creating a slew of designs that could be used whenever I needed a cute little bag. Both bags were designed in Illustrator and fed carefully through my printer. I scalloped the tops of the bags with a rotary cutter fitted with the scallop blade." Ullman's designs have a slightly antique feel and these bags look as if they might have been letterpress printed.

The guestroom favor bags (image 1) were inspired by an out-of-town guest's upcoming visit. "I purchased the muslin bags and then sewed the two custom labels to the front," Ullman says. "Inside were coordinating packets of hot cocoa and homemade marshmallows cut into the shape of snowflakes. Finding hot cocoa packets that matched our color scheme of yellow and gray proved to be quite a challenge. We ended up stumbling on these stunning single-serve packets at our local grocery store and bought as many as we could! They were the perfect find and fit brilliantly into the bags!"

1.

2.

---

1. Personal project
Hand sewing, hand finishing, hand assembly.

2. Personal project
Hand finishing, hand assembly.

BAGS GALLERY

Francisca Aldea Davila
Personal project
A low production cost was required for this bread packaging. Davila created the illustrations by hand first, then scanned them into the computer to refine them. The graphic was printed with inkjet onto handmade paper.

Peter Gregson Studio
Client: Aroma Food
The objective for this nut-packaging project was to create an eye-catching package that is both fun and communicative. Typography and graphic elements that look doodled over more traditional packaging add the whimsical aspect the client required.

Joanna Kee
Client: Come Home Soap
Simple stamps can have a big impact. For this edition of soap packaging, Kee applied stamps to small brown paper bags, folded down the opening, and applied round stickers on both sides of the bag before punching a hole through the layers and stringing a piece of baker's twine through the hole. The result is something with instant character and a bit of antique charm.

Peter Gregson Studio
Client: Woman Hairstyle Studio
An illustration of hair creates the pattern for these paper bags, which are used as packaging for hair products.

Project Party Studio
Client: Vanessa Espinosa
"There is a tradition in Spain that, before a wedding, someone close to the marrying couple brings a dozen eggs to the Clarissa Nuns who then pray for the weather to be beautiful on the day of the wedding," says designer Daniel Horacio Agostini. The designers of this wedding-egg packaging used fishnet and embellished tags of their design attached to the package with twine.

Subplot Design Inc.
Client: Petcurean Pet Nutrition
"Extensive research went into developing a realistic look and feel of a fresh market environment," says designer Ross Chandler. "The resulting imagery is a careful assembly of photographs and illustrations of real crinkled paper and burlap textures, overlaid with images of constructed market signage that inform the reader about the superior fresh ingredients."

REUSABLE
ELEMENTS
CASE STUDIES

CHAPTER 10 FABRICS AND WRAPS

Fabrics and wraps provide a wonderful opportunity for adding a tactile element to a package, and also for introducing pattern and color. By their nature, they add to the handmade aesthetic of any design.

SIDESHOW PRESS

Sideshow Press is a small letterpress shop in Charleston, South Carolina, USA. "On our noisy, pony-sized 1926 letterpress, we press and print each piece individually. Reactivating the vintage press is a labor-of-love collaboration of three women who've built careers around type, paper, found art, and design. We've been creating handcrafted letterpress goods since 2004. Housed under one roof, we design and press each piece in a shotgun storefront in historic downtown Charleston," says partner Amy Pastre.

"This project came about because eight of Charleston's finest chefs were invited to a private dinner party by our client, catered for by guest chef Barbara Lynch. Our client wanted a memorable, unique invitation. We packaged jars of lard (from Barbara Lynch's kitchen) as the invitation.

"Each jar was packaged by hand, labeled with letterpressed Kraft paper, wrapped with more Kraft paper, sealed with a second letterpressed label on Gmund gold paper, and tied with twine. Each invitation was accompanied by a personalized note from the host tucked into a small printed envelope. The packages were hand-delivered by a local butcher.

"The biggest challenge was making something unappealing—like lard—beautiful. Through the use of papers, materials, and printing techniques we sought to communicate the high-end nature of the event but still show the client's personality and close relationship with her invitees."

1.

1–3. Client: Kristin Newman Designs
Letterpress printing, hand assembly.

2.

3.

TUBBYPHUNK

Tubbyphunk is a compact but productive multi-disciplinary graphic design and communications studio in Middlesbrough, UK. The studio works closely with local, national, and international clients.

"The studio has developed a strong visual reputation for producing bespoke, distinctive, memorable, and effective creative solutions, adding value and immediate presence to businesses, products, and projects," says Creative Director Robert Page.

Tubbyphunk created this brochure for Cleveland College of Art & Design's Surface Pattern degree course to promote the college and showcase students' work. It was distributed at high-profile expos such as Indigo Paris and design shows in London and around the UK. "The concept was to create a 'wow' factor and a special emotional connection between the product and the recipient," says Page.

"The work produced by the students is extremely visual and made for great photography throughout the brochure. Coursework during the final weeks of school was documented photographically to create the catalog. I was particularly inspired by the old printing screens at the college, so I recycled the designs and textures to use for the external cardboard sleeve." The students formed a production line and individually hand-printed and glued the book sleeves. "This resulted in a book that reflected the hand-crafted nature of the students' work." The hand-assembled books were spiral-bound and then an invitation to the final exhibition was created using digital prints, brass eyelets, and jute string.

1.

1-3. Client: Cleveland College of Art
Screenprinting, hand assembly.

2.

3.

STITCH DESIGN CO.

Amy Pastre and Courtney Rowson, graphic designers with a knack for hands-on design, joined forces in 2009 to create a full-service design firm, Stitch Design Co. From their offices in downtown Charleston, South Carolina, USA, Stitch offers custom tailoring for design projects, large and small. "We're drawn to paper, texture, and type, and we bring a tactile sensibility to our projects. We use design to create solutions for clients across the country within arts and culture, fashion, food, consulting, publishing, and advertising. We love to work with innovative and interesting people who appreciate a collaborative approach and we are passionate about pushing ourselves to create the best possible work for them. With a made-to-order design

philosophy, we work with clients to develop brands and identity materials, and to craft the finest design for printed pieces, brochures, logos, advertising, and online and electronic media."

The duo came up with a fun way to send out client holiday gifts. "One of our favorite things to design are patterns," says Pastre. "I had a series of antique button samples from my grandmother that came out of a general store that she and my grandfather owned and operated for many years. The button cards had such a wonderful graphic quality that we wanted to capture that in a pattern used on wrapping paper for our holiday gifts. It was a challenge to translate the original button sample cards into the pattern. We tried to capture and

maintain the quirky quality of the different buttons. It was also a challenge to translate something three-dimensional, with patina and history, into something two-dimensional on the computer.

"We finished off the wrapping of the gifts with ribbon and personalized tags with a hand-sewn antique button. While the paper and tags were digitally printed, the hand finishing on each gift adds a personal touch."

1–2. Self promotion
Letterpress printing, screenprinting, hand-drawn illustrations, hand finishing.

ONE TRICK PONY

"Hammonton, New Jersey is the blueberry capital of the world," says Rob Reed, partner in the advertising agency One Trick Pony. "The day we moved into town and set up shop we noticed the sign and realized we had to take advantage of this in some way or another. We decided that if our clients weren't going to be able to come visit and sample a taste of Hammonton's second sweetest export, that we'd have to ship it to them. Each summer we send out more than 200 pints of fresh-picked Hammonton blueberries to clients across the country."

And each year, a contest is held among One Trick Pony staff to decide on the design of the wrapper. "We've done everything from letterpress to offset, handprinted, metallic inks, and even handmade buttons. The only constant is that the format is a simple sheet that can be wrapped around a pint of blueberries and easily glued." The blueberry wrappers have a distinctly handmade aesthetic. In the examples shown here, the typefaces mimic classic wood type, which lends an extra hand-crafted warmth to the designs.

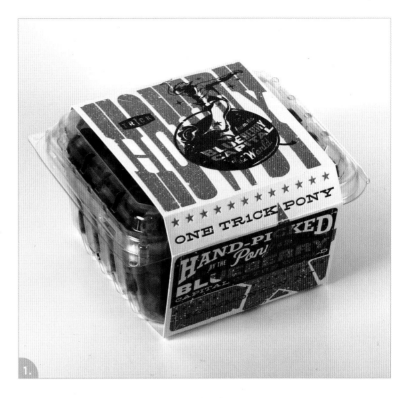

1-3. Self promotion
Letterpress printing, screenprinting, hand-drawn illustrations, hand finishing.

CHEWING THE CUD

Chewing the Cud is a design studio based in San Francisco, California, USA. "Our story is depicted in the media of paper and cloth; and the tale: a celebration of all things unique," says creator Viola Sutanto. "Our products are created with utmost care and thoughtfulness, using eco-friendly sources of the highest quality whenever possible."

The inspiration for Give Wraps™ came from the Japanese furoshiki, a traditional wrapping cloth used to transport clothing, food, and gifts. "This is a modern take on the furoshiki, which is commonly made of silk or chirimen crepe, and embellished or dyed in different colors. Ours is made from cotton. The form is the same (i.e. an oversized square cloth), but the design, the material, as well as the idea of conveying a 'Give' message on the knotted ends when wrapped, is our interpretation and evolution of the traditional furoshiki. We wanted the final product to be both functional and inspirational—functional because it serves as an eco-friendly alternative to conventional wrapping paper and is reusable for various purposes, and inspirational because the Give Wrap™ itself serves as a thoughtful way of gift giving," says Sutanto.

"We started by brainstorming on the idea of gift giving. We then looked into the visual language and symbolism of gift giving, which varied so much across cultures. Coincidentally, my thesis (from years ago) in art school was focused on gifts and gift giving, so I already had some sketches and ideas that came full circle. We infused meaning into each style with graphics that spoke to the idea of giving. A cluster of good luck symbols resulted in a striking design that spoke of giving luck. In another style, whimsical tree illustrations became the metaphor for giving wisdom—the perfect choice for wrapping books.

1.

1-4. Client: EVO
Screenprinting, upcycling.

"There was a lot of good old hand-sketching, and experimentation with different fabrics and folding techniques in the process. We knew we wanted to work with 100% organic cotton and the printing to be done with soy-based inks, so sourcing was a challenge. The first priority was to find a manufacturing partner who was not only set up to work with large screens (our wraps are 28 x 28in/70 x 70cm), but also committed to working with sustainable materials and producing high-quality products in a fair manner.

Since we are a small studio with limited resources, we were only able to start with a small sampling of designs, which is not cost-effective in terms of production. The entire process was, and still is, a learning experience, but well worth it!

"The art of cloth-wrapping is inherently 'imperfect' due to the nature of fabrics and folds. It can never be perfectly duplicated, much like hand-drawn illustrations. Every fold and every line is a result of the human touch."

FABRICS AND WRAPS GALLERY

Jesse Harris
Academic work
"For this concept for packaging for a fishmonger, I used both hand-drawn and computer-drawn sketches of fish parts and fillets from photos I had taken for research, and translated these into cut-paper shapes. These shapes had an interesting and original aesthetic. I loved them so much, I translated them into a traditional printed form by screenprinting them onto different papers and materials used to wrap the fish," says Harris.

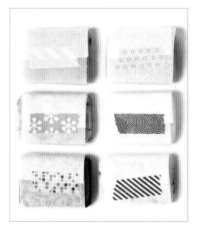

Janell Anderson
Personal project
Anderson used materials she had on hand, including Japanese washi tape and paper, to wrap her soaps individually by hand for her company Prunella Soaps. The design is simple, but graphically interesting, and its simplicity reflects the purity of her handmade soaps.

Vadim Paschenko
Client: Candy Lights
Paschenko printed on thin tissue paper for this handmade-candle packaging. He then embellished each wrapped product individually with stickers, wax, and twine.

Summer Watkins, with Desiree Mortimore
(photographer: Jenny Liu)
Personal project
Unwanted sweaters can be easily made into wonderful presentation sleeves for bottles of wine, as seen in this fantastic example of recycling.

Summer Watkins , with Desiree Mortimore
(photographer: Jenny Liu)
Personal project
Stylist Summer Watkins gave some gift packaging a special touch with items she already had. "Besides a few extra pieces of pom-pom trim and lace, most of the fabric was pulled from my own collection of leftovers. I almost never throw away fabric and even recycle old blouses or sweaters that I no longer wear for these kinds of projects. When you choose a simple color palette like this, you have the opportunity to really focus on texture, which is one of my favorite elements."

Stitch Design Co.
Client: Lowcountry Local First
These invitations were printed letterpress on reusable cloth produce bags using three colors. A mailing tag was sewn onto the bag so it could be mailed directly to doorsteps.

CHAPTER 11 RECYCLED AND UPCYCLED

This chapter looks not only at packaging that uses recycled or recyclable materials, but also at those that repurpose existing products, often providing a cheaper, and unique, alternative to other sustainable packaging options.

OFFICE

Office is a creative studio based in San Francisco, California, USA. "We craft strategies and design experiences to make things better," says Studio Manager Julie Dyer.

eBay asked Office to develop a new set of shipping boxes as part of a pilot program to help make shipping a little greener. The company planned to give away 100,000 of the boxes to eBay sellers, then encourage the recipients to reuse them.

"According to eBay, if each box gets used five times, the program could protect nearly 4,000 trees, save 2.4 million gallons of water, and conserve enough electricity to power 49 homes for a year. To inspire people to reuse the boxes, we needed to tell that story in an engaging way," says Dyer.

In accordance with eBay's visual language, Office developed friendly illustrations that have a hand-drawn aesthetic, and copy that emphasizes the potential benefits to the planet and includes tips for greener packing. A happy little bird asks "Where to next?" and, to track each box's journey, there's space allowed to write a note to the next person to receive it, so they can see just how far it has come.

 1–3. Client: eBay
Recycled materials, water-based inks.

Although it wasn't part of the project brief, Office also worked with the box manufacturer and printer to develop an environmentally friendly solution. Each eBay box is made with 100% recycled content, printed with water-based inks, and designed to require minimal tape. Once it reaches the end of its useful shipping life, it is fully recyclable. Printed on the box is the following text: "Don't worry, it will come back as something nice, like a birthday card or movie-theater popcorn bag."

"The biggest challenge for this project was a tight timeline," says Dyer. "There really wasn't time for us, or for our client, to second-guess anything... We worked fast and it was produced fast. Sometimes fun, fresh ideas can be stalled by over-thinking; fortunately, that wasn't the case here."

2.

3.

STITCH DESIGN CO.

Rewined candles are all-natural soy wax candles poured into discarded wine bottles. "They have a family of intoxicating scents that are all designed to mimic flavors and aromas you find in your favorite varietals of wines," says Amy Pastre of Stitch Design Co. (see also page 156.) "The client came to us looking to enhance his current packaging. We redesigned his logo using hand-drawn type and redesigned his Kraft-paper labels with simple typography and a layered labeling system. Each candle has a vintage and producer label, and is signed and dated by the candle maker. A wood-veneer wax topper sits on top of the candle to keep it clean and free of dust before use. We also developed a color system using wax seals to color-code each varietal scent and finished off the packaging with a small green sticker reminding each purchaser to please recycle again. To top it all off, each label was letterpressed by Sideshow Press and hand applied, making these candles truly unique and hand-crafted."

"One of the aspects of this project that makes it so unique is the fact that we used multiple processes and materials," says Pastre. The main label is letterpress-printed on Kraft label stock. The "producer" label is offset-printed and the wax seals are part of a family of colors. Each label and seal is layered on the bottle (which has beautiful color and texture all its own). "We worked closely with the client to ensure this layer technique would be labor-friendly on his end. We were excited that he was willing to put more effort into assembly to make a big impact with the finished project."

1–4. Client: Rewined
Letterpress printing, hand-drawn type, hand assembly.

2.

3.

4.

THREE BLIND ANTS

Three Blind Ants is owned by husband-and-wife team Aaron and Ami Opsal, who created Boxsal. Aaron is an advertising, branding, and design veteran and owner of The Brand Hatchery, a branding, advertising, design, and interactive firm.

"Boxsal is an eco-friendly, modern picnic box dressed head-to-toe in a design style that allows you to tailor your picnic to your personal style. Whether it's the romantic taste of Today's Date, the inner-city style of Urban Picnic, or the casual coolness of Office Escape, Boxsal is a place to pack your creativity along with some tasty treats," explains Aaron.

Each Boxsal is completely recyclable and biodegradable, right down to the knives, forks, and spoons included in the Boxsal Eatin' Tool Set. Utensils and cups are made of compostable corn starch. The trays and bowls are created from sugar-cane fiber. Each set also contains recycled napkins and a compostable trash bag for your picnic leftovers. And while the Eatin' Tool Set is disposable, the picnic box can be used over and over. It can even double as a storage box, luggage, or portfolio case in the winter months. "The fact that each picnic box is fully sustainable was kind of a given for the project. We figured that was really just the entry fee associated with fabricating a new product these days. The real magic lies in the creativity that each Boxsal can bring to a picnic. This is an industry that hasn't seen any giant leaps forward in a really long time. You no longer need a 100-year old oak tree to serve as the cornerstone of your afternoon getaway. Instead, you can find the nearest rooftop or inner-city park and toss down a blanket and some imagination," says Aaron.

1-4. Personal project
Hand-drawn and hand-painted illustrations, hand assembly.

All of the illustrations were hand drawn prior to being scanned in. "For the Urban Picnic Box, we worked with a local graffiti artist to sketch up the panel artwork," Aaron says. "We tested a few spray-painted options, a few ink-and-brushstroke style applications, and some good-ole-fashion pencil sketches. We ended up using a combination of all three styles to create the final artwork. The creative war room [where they work] is about 20 x 16 x 16ft (6 x 5 x 5m) and almost every square inch of it was covered in sketches. We divided all the designs up by markets and started our editing process. And since we were on a start-up budget, we looked at what we were able to design in-house. We wanted to do ten products to start with, but the budget made that edit for us pretty quickly. The three current designs target three different audiences. Urban [see image 1] is for the guys and all the inner-city crowd. Today's Date [see image 2] is romantic and it's really fun for kids. And Office Escape [see images 3 and 4] is for corporate-America culture.

"The Today's Date paint-by-numbers was a blast to create," he continues. "We grabbed some old family photos and wallpaper scraps, which we collaged together and used as the inspiration. We freehanded the initial sketches at half-scale, then transferred them to the computer. We even colored one of the first prototypes with French Gray markers to ensure all the paint-by-number color scales worked. It took about a day to color in."

All of the Eatin' Tool Sets and tags are hand-assembled, and the Boxsal picnic boxes are hand-assembled in a local warehouse. All Boxsals are printed and produced locally in Dallas/Fort Worth, Texas, USA. The stock is a 60% post-consumer, FSC grade, corrugated board printed with Earthflex inks. Aaron explains, "Soy-based inks didn't give us the density and coverage we needed, so Earthflex was a great sustainable alternative. We use a traditional flex printing method and die-cut for the shape."

2.

3.

4.

ERIC KASS

Eric Kass (see also page 152) is the founder of Funnel: The Fine Commercial Art Practice of Eric Kass, a multi-disciplinary art and design studio in Indianapolis, Indiana, USA.

Linnea's Lights™ candles combine all-natural soy wax, lead-free cotton candle wicks, pure essences, and fine fragrances to create clean-burning, highly aromatic candles. All Linnea's Lights™ natural soy candles are meticulously hand-poured in small batches. Custom die-cut uncoated labels were printed using offset lithography in one PMS metallic with scent names hand rubber-stamped in various colors to correspond to the particular aroma, adding a variety of colors, and expressing the handmade nature of the product while providing a cost-effective way to designate ever-changing fragrances. The basic packaging materials relate to the purity of the product, while the ornate detail of the old-world package-inspired design communicates a sophisticated attention to quality. Cardboard boxes are a cost-effective and highly recyclable method of packaging.

"The challenge was to create a very sophisticated, high-end-feeling package with the tight budget of a start-up that also could be easily customized on the fly to accommodate an endless variety of ever-changing scents," says Kass.

1.

2.

3.

 1-3. Client: Linnea's Lights™
Hand stamping, hand pouring, hand packaging.

MANGION & LIGHTFOOT

Mangion & Lightfoot is a design company based on the Mediterranean island of Malta, formed as a partnership between designers Matthew Mangion and Mark Lightfoot. They provide strategy, creativity, and implementation to support their clients' brands.

This particular project came about when a good client and friend, Winston Zahra, brought a label-less bottle of homemade olive oil produced from his own grove to a meeting as a gift to the fellows. They then discussed the idea of coming up with some sort of environmentally friendly labeling system for the oil. "The main challenge of the project was to produce a label that minimized the use of industrial processes and find a process that would not be too labor-intensive for the quantity of the product," says Mangion. The constraints of having to use recycled materials, he says, inspired the use of newspapers and bits of cardboard that would provide the base of the label. The next problem was how to communicate the product information on the "scrap" paper. Since product quantities were fairly low (in the hundreds) they came up with the idea of having a set of rubber stamps. The set includes a logo stamp, an authenticity stamp, stamps for the volume of the bottle, etc. Rubber stamps provide an eco-friendly, cost-effective, and efficient way to transmit information on the bottle.

The base of the label was created by attaching broadsheet newspapers together to form a large sheet. Using a large ruler and a pen, the label sizes were drawn out, and the bits of cardboard were then added to each label to provide a clear base for the information (rather than rubber-stamping the newspaper, which would take away from the clarity of the information). The labels were then rubber-stamped, cut, and glued to the bottles. The whole process is done by hand.

4. Client: Winston Zahra
Handmade labels, hand stamped, hand finished.

ELEA LUTZ

Nostalgia Organics is a toiletries and giftware company that began as a labor of love, says creator Elea Lutz. Pairing her lifelong passion for art, design, and anything of sentimental value with her interest in essential oils, botanicals, and natural health creates the union at the heart of the brand. Lutz created the packaging design herself. "Much of my inspiration comes from my childhood and the sensations and simplicities of my grandmother's homespun world: watching my grandmother tend to the garden, sew ruffles on a dress, or mail a hand-written letter. I find comfort and inspiration in these small, modest details of my past. I'm also inspired by my children. You'll find their funny pictures, little toys, or handmade doodles sprinkled about the studio."

Lutz designs all of the patterns and labels herself. "I usually sketch out ideas on paper and then work digitally to color and fine-tune, but the process is determined by the project—the look and feel I'm trying to achieve." Lutz says she worked through various packaging and design ideas (sampling packaging, components, color combinations, etc.), often spending months designing each concept. "I wanted the packaging to have a comforting, old-world feel drawing back to my inspiration," she says. "I also wanted the line to overflow with fine details—hand stitches, ribbons, and luxurious materials.

1-5. Personal project
Hand-drawn illustrations, hand assembled.

3.

4.

5.

"One of my biggest challenges was to create packaging with the same care and concern as the organic ingredients inside. Reusable, recyclable, sustainable—all of these qualities were at the top of my priority list. It can be difficult, especially on a limited budget, to find suitable packaging that meets these requirements. I had to think way outside the box.

In the end, I was able to source beautiful, 100% post-consumer-recycled paper for packaging and labels. The challenge also inspired me to develop reusable fabric packaging with labels that unfold to reveal sewing patterns. The patterns can be used with the fabric to create something new and useful from the packaging rather than discarding it."

Lutz adds, "As I continue to develop new products, I still prioritize reusable, recyclable, sustainable qualities in the packaging. It's difficult, but staying true to the core of the brand is important and worth the challenge."

LINDSAY PERKINS

Lindsay Perkins is a freelance designer living in Savannah, Georgia, USA, where she graduated from Savannah College of Art and Design with a degree in graphic design. She created this thoughtful approach to sustainable design while still a student.

The branding and packaging concept was inspired by a small, local, organic farm in rural Maine. The idea was to design sustainable, organic, label-free packaging. The phrase "The grass is greener on our side" inspired the packaging concept. The paper used for the bag and menus is 100% recycled and biodegradable, made with grass seeds so, however it is disposed of, wherever it ends up, grass will grow.

All type used in the packaging is hand-rendered to resemble grass. The milk bottles, label-free, have all the information printed directly onto the glass, and would be returned by the customer to be refilled and reused. The cheeses are packaged with biodegradable cheesecloth and wax paper. Different cheeses are distinguished by a sticker that also holds the wax paper together. All packages are hand-stamped with the farm logo so the reproduction on each is just a little bit different, just like the produce from an organic farm.

1.

2.

3.

1–3. Academic work
Hand-drawn type, hand-drawn illustration, hand finished, hand stamped.

RECYCLED AND UPCYCLED GALLERY

Chris Piascik
Client: Morgan & Milo

Chris Piascik worked with Moth Design and Alphabet Arm to illustrate shoe boxes for Morgan & Milo, a children's shoe company located in Boston, Massachusetts, USA. The Kraft boxes, screenprinted with white and green, are designed to promote recycling and encourage the end user to keep the box. They are covered with puzzles, games, mazes, riddles, quotes, and fun characters.

Khadia Ulumbekova
Academic work

The illustration and packaging for this selection of teas was inspired by the traditional art of Sri Lanka. The illustration was done by hand. "I drew it on paper with acrylic paints. To create the aged effect I used silkscreening, then scanned my image and, because I printed it on Kraft paper, the result was a bit mottled, giving it the overall desired effect of an old, worn printed illustration," says Ulumbekova.

Chris Chapman
Academic work

"Plastics have revolutionized the food industry—from fruit to pasta, we have wrapped this incredibly versatile material around almost everything we eat... It has not only allowed us to increase our food production, but has also created a vastly delocalized food network," says Chris Chapman. "This experimental packaging design attempts to reduce these factors through the material's inherent properties. I chose to use traditional meat paper combined with more modern starch-coated cards to prevent unsightly damp spots. The packages are also intentionally designed for hand assembly to help prevent large-scale or excessive manufacture, forcing producers to focus on the quality of their product rather than its quantity."

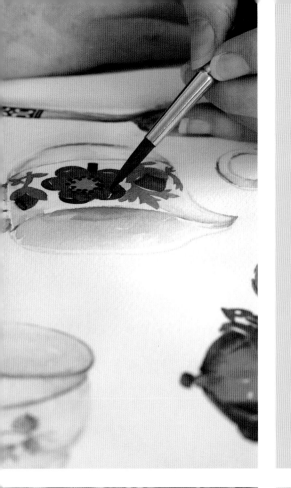

GOING PRO
TUTORIALS
AND PROFILES

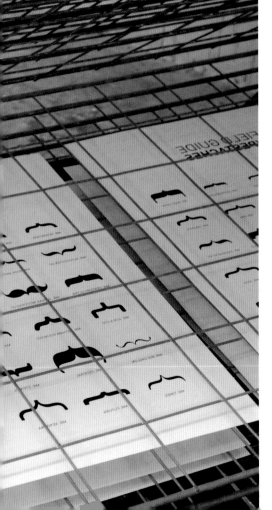

CHAPTER 12 PRACTICAL SKILLS

There are practical skills needed to bring packaging designs to life. The tutorials in this chapter give you the basic tools required—creating a repeat pattern and a box template, and using Illustrator's 3D capabilities—and introduce the techniques of letterpress, block, and screenprinting.

CREATING A REPEATING PATTERN

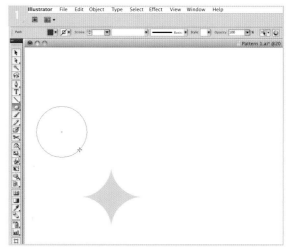

This tutorial explains a fairly quick method of making a seamless or repeating pattern in Adobe Illustrator. As with most things in the Adobe suite of programs, a seamless pattern can be made in many other ways. A Google search will reveal a good range of tutorials, some simple, some with more precise measurements and calculations. The method outlined here falls somewhere between the two.

Creating elements
Open a new document in Illustrator. I used regular letter-size paper dimensions. Either create some shapes directly in your document or copy them from another document and paste them in (select, then Cmd + V).

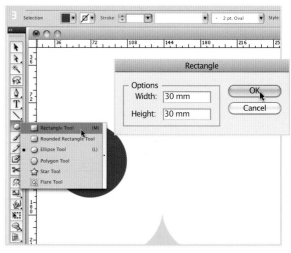

Setting up your document
Make sure you have your rulers showing (Cmd + R), that you've got Snap to Point checked (View > Snap to Point), and that your guides are unlocked (View > Guides > uncheck Lock Guides), as you will need to move the guides later on.

Establishing your background square
Using a square for the base unit of your pattern will make it easier to align your shapes to create a successful repeat. Create a square by clicking on the Rectangle tool and then double-clicking on your artboard: a Dialog box will pop up. Type into this the dimensions you want for your square. I used 30 × 30mm (c. 1¹/₄ × 1¹/₄in).

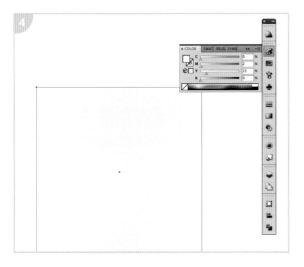

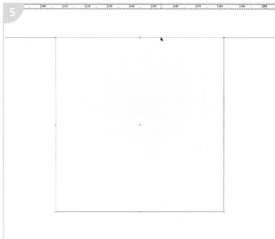

Filling your background square

You can fill the square with a color or keep it transparent, but make sure it doesn't have an outline. When you come to repeat this square to form your pattern, an outline would show and break up what you want to be a continuous background.

Setting your guides

Click on your Rulers to drag guides onto the edges of your square.

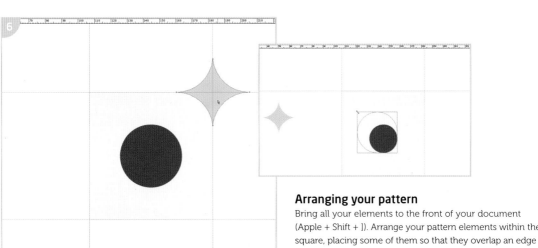

Arranging your pattern

Bring all your elements to the front of your document (Apple + Shift +]). Arrange your pattern elements within the square, placing some of them so that they overlap an edge of the square. I scaled up some of my original elements to better fill my square. If you need to scale up or down, select the element and drag from the corner while holding down the Shift button: this will keep the proportions of your element intact.

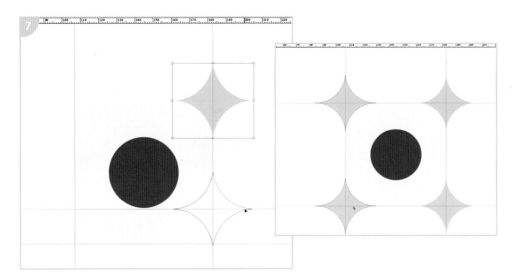

Making the pattern "seamless"

Here's where the "seamless" comes in. You need to match up each element that overlaps the square—above, below, and to each side—so that the pattern flows without interruption. Select one overlapping element, along with the guide it overlaps. Holding down the Shift and Option keys, drag the guide and element to the opposite side of the square. Holding down both keys simultaneously will allow you to duplicate the items you are moving and keep them in line with their originals. Duplicate and move each overlapping element horizontally, vertically, or both, as necessary. Because my element overlaps both the top and right edges of the square, it is necessary for me to duplicate it both horizontally and vertically, to all four corners of the square.

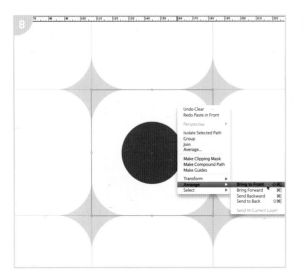

Creating a bounding box

Create a copy (Apple + C) of the base square, then lock your base square (Apple + 2). Go to Paste in Place (Apple + Shift + V) to paste your copy of the square in position.

Preparing to crop

Now you need to convert your pattern to a swatch. First hide your guides (Apple + ;), then unlock your background square (Apple + Alt + 2).

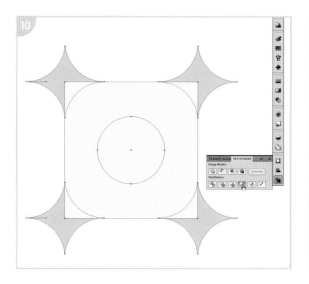

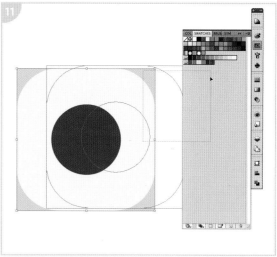

Cropping

Select all your elements, open the Pathfinder palette (Window > Pathfinder), and hit the Crop button (the fourth button down in the Pathfinder palette).

Saving your swatch

You should now have a cropped square. Drag this square into the Swatches panel.

Testing your swatch

Test your pattern by making a rectangular or square shape and filling it with repeats of your new swatch. Check that the elements tessellate correctly where they repeat, to give one continuous pattern.

USING ADOBE ILLUSTRATOR'S 3D CAPABILITIES

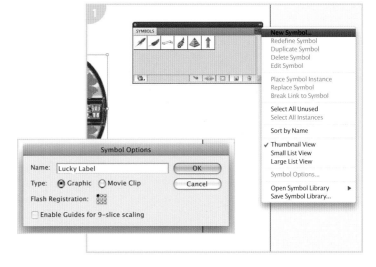

This tutorial shows how to use Illustrator's 3D capabilities to create a bottle prototype, complete with a custom label, using the 3D Revolve effect. This allows you to revolve an outline profile of the right side of an object around a central axis to create a 3D object. Once you have the profile of the object you want to create, you can revolve it, add lighting, and map other elements onto it relatively quickly. When you get the hang of it, you can create all sorts of 3D packaging substrates, such as cans, boxes, and cartons.

Preparing your label

Before creating the bottle, ensure your label is ready to be applied. To prepare artwork to wrap around a 3D object, you need first to make it a symbol. First, select the label and outline all the text (Cmd + Shift + O or Type > Create Outlines), then select the artwork using the selection tool. Open the Symbols palette (Window > Symbols) and drag the artwork into the pallete. Alternatively, select the artwork and, under the flyout menu of the Symbols palette, select New Symbol, name it, and click OK. In the Dialog box that appears, make sure you save the symbol as a graphic and not a movie clip.

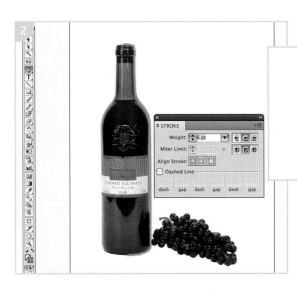

Tracing your bottle

Now you need to create the profile of the bottle. You can draw this freehand or trace around a photograph. I found a simple image to trace on clipart.com. Because you're going to revolve around a central axis, you only need to create the right half of the profile by tracing with the Pen tool. Make sure the open end of your profile is to the left, as shown. I used a 6pt stroke to make it clear enough for me to see, and to mimic the thickness of the glass in a bottle. Use the Rounded Caps and Rounded Joins in the Strokes palette so that your bottle doesn't appear to have any sharp edges.

Creating your contour

Now that you have a profile, you need to give it a color that mimics a bottle. I chose a deep green. With the 3D Revolve Options Dialog box open (Effect > 3D > Revolve), select More Options. Click the Shading Color tab and the Color Picker menu will pop up. Mix and set your new color, then click OK for both the color picker and 3D Revolve Options Dialog boxes to apply the new color.

Converting your contour

Once the stroked contour is as you want it, you'll need to convert it to an outline so that you can make it a Filled Path without altering its shape. To turn the Stroke into an outline, select it, then go to Object > Expand. A Dialog box will pop up. Make sure both Fill and Stroke are selected, then click OK.

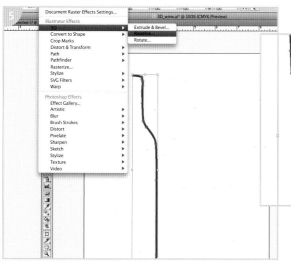

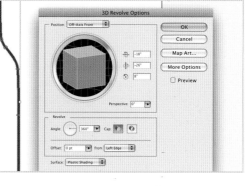

Revolving the contour

Spin your bottle profile using Illustrator's 3D Revolve effect. Select the profile and go to Effect > 3D > Revolve. Leave the default settings in the Dialog window that pops up, click Preview, and watch your profile become a bottle.

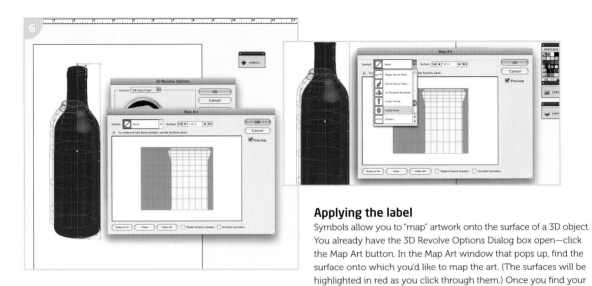

Applying the label

Symbols allow you to "map" artwork onto the surface of a 3D object. You already have the 3D Revolve Options Dialog box open—click the Map Art button. In the Map Art window that pops up, find the surface onto which you'd like to map the art. (The surfaces will be highlighted in red as you click through them.) Once you find your surface, select the symbol you want to map onto it.

Placing the symbol

Drag the symbol into position (a white background indicates areas that will be visible; a shaded background areas that won't). In the Map Art window check Preview so you can see what happens as you move or resize your label. You can resize it by dragging corner points in the bounding box and holding down the Shift key to maintain proportions. Check Shade Artwork to shade the label with the same lighting as your bottle. Click OK in the Map Art window and OK again in the 3D Revolve Options box when you've got everything looking as it should.

Adding a neck wrap

For this bottle, I also added a neck wrap from another label I had created. I turned it into a symbol and mapped it onto the bottle in the same way as for the main label.

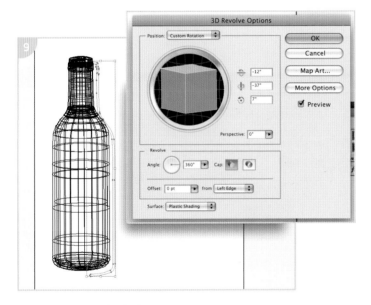

Final tweaks and printing

If you want to tweak your bottle, select it and open your 3D Revolve Options Dialog box (Effect > 3D > Revolve). A cube will appear in the pop-up window: you can turn your bottle in space by clicking and dragging the edges of the cube or the ring around the cube. You can also change the perspective of the bottle or alter the lighting, as previously mentioned. Once you are happy with your creation, print.

PREPARING FILES FOR LETTERPRESS PRINTING

Below are some basic guidelines to help you set up files and prepare them for letterpress printing. Designing for letterpress comes with its own set of considerations and guidelines. It is best to talk with your letterpress printer prior to setting up files in order to establish how they like files to be formatted and delivered. If you are designing in Illustrator, you should have each color set on its own layer when your design is completed. For this reason it is best either to design first in black and then create each color layer separately, or to design with your palette and use your software to create the color separations for you.

Color

Use only spot colors in your document, not RGB or CMYK. Keep the number of colors you use to a minimum, and don't use any screens or shades. The colors in your document should correspond to the ink your printer will be using; if they will be printing using two inks, use only two spot colors throughout your document.

Fonts

It's best to avoid using type smaller than 6pt as any smaller than this won't hold detail and will be hard to read. If you are using Illustrator (do not use Photoshop to set type as it does not allow for all the control and fine-tuning that Illustrator does), outline all text before submitting your artwork. If you have a script font with very thin lines, check with the printer regarding how well the font will print, or whether it will print at all.

Images

Vector images from Illustrator work wonderfully when letterpressed, as do TIFFs. Avoid using JPGs as they won't give the clarity of line required.

Convert any Photoshop images into Bitmap mode: Photoshop images are made up of tiny dots of color (halftone) rather than solid color. To do this open Photoshop, select Image > Mode > Grayscale, then Image > Mode > Bitmap. For your bitmap files use a resolution of 600—1200dpi and 50% threshold. For faster images (from Photoshop), avoid the grayscale color mode—use a 1200dpi bitmap instead.

Embed all linked images (Links palette > Embed Link) in Illustrator. If you use Quark XPress or InDesign, be sure to include the image files.

Lines

Line widths should be .25pt or thicker.

Trim size

Show the final trim size of your document using a 1pt, 100% CMYK black border. Some printers will also allow you to show final trim size by setting the document to trim size. Check with your printer to get his or her preference.

1.

1. A type case, whence come the terms "uppercase" and "lowercase." Each compartment holds a different letter, with capitals in the upper case and lowercase in the lower. Image courtesy of Typoretum http://www.typoretum.co.uk

2.

Dies and scores

Die cuts should be clearly indicated with a 1pt 100% magenta line; scores should be indicated with a 1pt 100% cyan line.

Bleeds

If you are using a bleed, extend your artwork at least $^1/_{16}$in (1.6mm) beyond the trim.

Solid colors

Blocks of solid color print differently on letterpress than with conventional printing methods such as digital or offset. While letterpress does lay down a thick film of ink, the process tends to show the texture of the sheet, resulting in a slightly "suede" look, whereas colors appear more evenly saturated with conventional printing. Also, solid areas do not give the appearance of depth that fine type and thin lines do.

2. These cards by printmaker Jesse Breytenbach were designed in conjunction with letterpress printers Planet Press. Her pen-and-ink drawings were scanned and vectorized for printing on a Heidelberg platen press.

CREATING A DIELINE

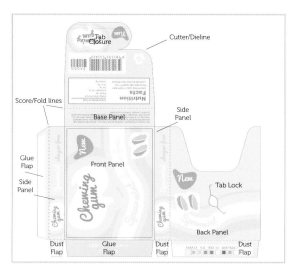

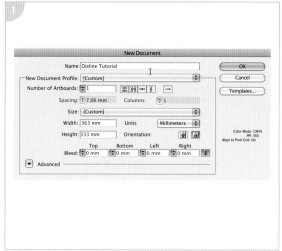

This tutorial explains the basics of dielines and how to create one in Illustrator from a pre-existing package. For this tutorial, I used a small gum pack. A dieline is a flattened outline of the cut and fold lines for a package; it serves as a template. Designers often receive dielines from their printer; however, if your client wants a new style of package or a package structure for which the printer does not have a template, you might need to create one from scratch. If the client gives you a package to use, it's pretty easy to scan it in and create dielines over it in a program such as Illustrator.

Setting up your file
Create a new file in Illustrator big enough to hold your dieline, PMS swatches, and design notes.

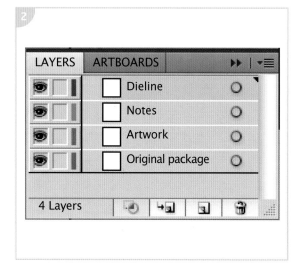

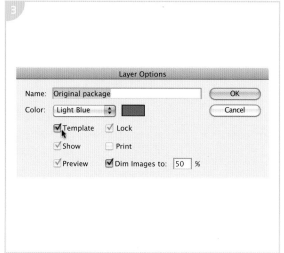

Creating layers
Create four layers: one titled "Dieline", one "Artwork," one "Original package" and one "Notes." Your Dieline layer should be on top.

Make a template layer
When you create the Original package layer, check the Template option. This will allow you to always see the original packaging, but as a light tint so that you can clearly see your dieline and new artwork in the foreground.

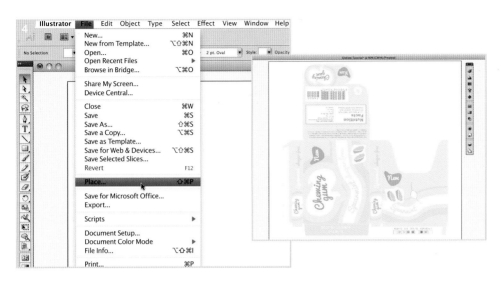

Placing your artwork

For this small template, I used an 11 × 8½in (28 × 21.6cm) artboard. Gently open out your package and scan it. Place this scan on the Original package layer and then lock that layer by clicking on the padlock icon.

Drawing lines

Use either Shapes or the Pen tool, whichever you are most comfortable with, to draw your guidelines. Either is fine, as long as you are making clean, accurate lines.

Check measurements

When you work from a pre-existing template, you'll need to check your accuracy by taking measurements from your template and comparing them to the in-progress dieline.

Cut lines

Cut lines are indicated with solid red lines, typically .25 or .50pt.

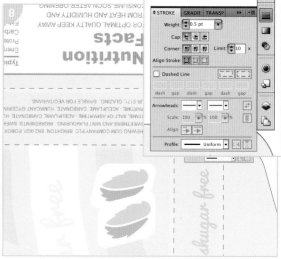

Fold lines

Folds are indicated with solid or dotted red lines.
(I use dotted lines in this tutorial.)

Safe margin lines

Safe margins are shown either with guides or blue lines.

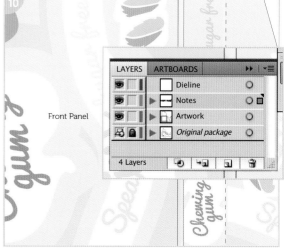

Labels

Identifying labels, such as "Front Panel," "Glue Panel," "Tuck Flap,"
etc., should be put on your Notes layer.

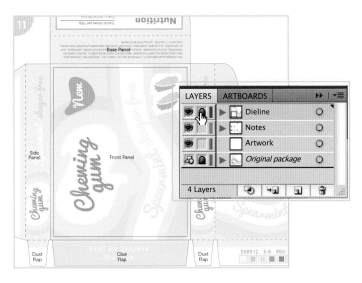

Lock Original package layer

Once you have created your dielines, lock that layer by clicking
the padlock icon.

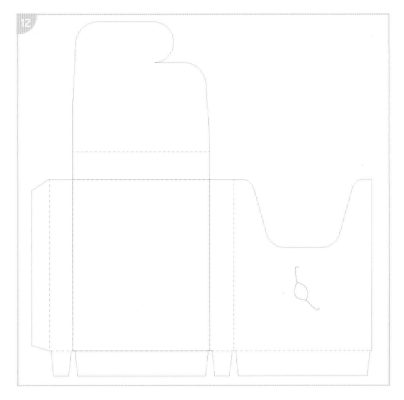

Creating a prototype

Once you have a basic dieline, you can
place your art on the Artwork layer. Create
a hardcopy prototype of your package by
printing out and assembling your design.
This will show you any errors in orientation,
measurement, text or art placement
and give you the opportunity to fix them.

Once your dieline is ready, send it to the
printer and ask for a proof. If you receive this
in digital rather than printed form, print and
assemble it in order to check one last time
for orientation, spelling, placement errors,
and so on. If you can't print out your dieline
to full size, assembling a miniature version
will work as, by this point, your
measurements should be perfect.

SCREENPRINTING

For this tutorial, I printed in a studio with an exposure unit. If you're printing from home, there are many online tutorials that show you how to set up a home exposure unit with a photoflood bulb. This screenprinting tutorial is adapted from a guide created by Rachel Lackey of Green Pea Press. Techniques were demonstrated by Graham Carter at Boxbird gallery (www.Boxbird.co.uk), with photography by Ivan Jones.

Screens

When choosing a screen, you'll need to consider the mesh count (the tightness of the weave of the fabric). What you need will depend on the substrate onto which you'll be printing. The higher the mesh count, the closer the fibers of the mesh are; a lower mesh count means a looser weaving, which allows more ink to pass through the screen. For optimal results when printing on paper, use a mesh count of 230, which will allow you to print finer details and thinner lines. A fabric substrate will be more absorbent, so a lower mesh count is appropriate. Screens with a mesh count of 110 or 160 will work well. A mesh count of 180 allows for both paper and fabric printing.

Before you get started, it is important to note which side of the screen is which. The back of the screen is the side on which the screen and the metal or wood of the frame are flush. It is referred to as the printing or paper side. The front (which is the side that will be facing up when you are printing) is the recessed side; it is referred to as the squeegee side.

Always check your screen for tears and holes. Repair any damage with a drop of superglue and a small piece of duct tape on either side of the screen. Hold the screen up to a light source to check for emulsion or ink residue, and clean any you find using emulsion remover. Ensure your screen is large enough for the image you want to make, leaving a margin of at least 2in (5cm) around the inside of the frame.

Emulsion

Emulsion is what you use to make your stencil on the screen. In areas where the emulsion hardens (which will occur when you expose it to light), the screen becomes blocked, preventing ink from passing through the screen during printing. In unexposed areas the emulsion remains soft—you will eventually wash this off the screen. The ink will pass through those areas of the screen during printing to produce your print.

You can apply the emulsion with either a scoop coater or a squeegee. A scoop coater is a specialized tool that holds emulsion and allows you to apply a smooth, even coat of it to your screen. The squeegee is the messier option, because it doesn't hold emulsion. Either option is fine, but if you are new to screenprinting, it might be easier to use a scoop coater.

To mix your emulsion put on your gloves, then follow the directions on the photo emulsion bottle. (Following the instructions on my emulsion bottle, I half-filled the bottle of sensitizer with cold water and dissolved the paste completely before pouring the whole solution into the emulsion container and mixing thoroughly.)

Resources
Hobby Lobby
www.hobbylobby.com
Carries Speedball brand products for water-based screenprinting at home, including an emulsion kit, plastic squeegee, and some fabric inks.

Dick Blick
www.dickblick.com
A good resource for small-scale screenprinting. Carries all supplies, chemicals, inks, etc. The website shows some "how-to" videos for simple processes/projects.

Silk Screening Supplies.com
www.silkscreeningsupplies.com
A good resource for large-scale screenprinting and Plastisol inks supplies. They have good, detailed descriptions for each product and its use, as well as several "how-to" videos.

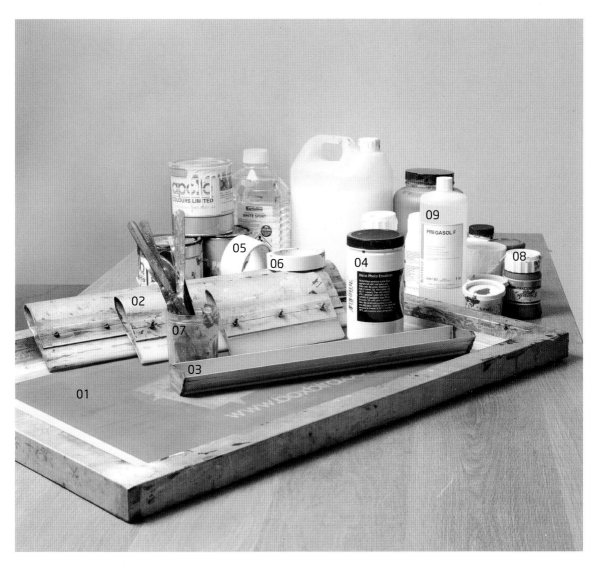

Materials

Essential equipment for screenprinting:
- a clean screen (01)
- a squeegee or scoop coater (02)
- a coating trough (03)
- photo emulsion (04)
- water-resistant tape (05)
- masking tape (06)
- mixing sticks or palette knives (07)
- inks and other media (08)
- a stencil strip (09)

Optional materials and equipment:
- rubber or latex gloves
- a dark drying area
- transparencies
- an exposure unit
- a washout area
- spray adhesive
- a printing station
- a flash dryer or heat gun

Coating your screen

Your squeegee or scoop coater should span almost the total width of your screen, but still fit easily inside your screen frame without getting stuck. Before you start, check your squeegee or scoop coater for nicks or other damage. Any flaw on the thin edge will give you an uneven application of emulsion. If you are using a squeegee, apply a line of emulsion across the top of the screen, then pull it down over the screen toward you with the blade of the squeegee. If you are using a scoop coater, fill it about halfway with photo emulsion, taking care to pour over the rounded edge of the scoop coater. Replace the lid on the emulsion container immediately, and tightly.

Prop or hold your screen with one hand, tilted at a gentle angle, and place the thin edge of your squeegee or scoop coater flat against it, about 1in (2.5cm) above the bottom frame. Pull the scoop firmly upward to apply a thin coat of emulsion to the screen, tilting the squeegee/scoop back before pulling it away at the top of the screen: this will help to avoid drips. Flip the screen over and repeat on the other side. Do not try to apply emulsion all the way to the edges of your screen; you won't be able to print those areas anyway, and it usually makes a mess. Leave a margin of about 1in (2.5cm) all around.

After coating both sides, pull the thin edge of the scoop up both sides of the screen firmly to thin out and smooth the emulsion, then apply another layer of emulsion to both sides of the screen and smooth again. There should be no drips, streaks, lines, or hairs. Continue smoothing both sides of the screen until all irregularities have been cleared.

Drying your emulsion

Place the coated screen in a dark, dry place such as a closet or cabinet. The actual screen should not be touching anything. Some people lean the screen up against a wall or cabinet as it dries, while others prefer to keep it horizontal, and prop it up by the four corners using anything they have to hand. A fan will help to circulate air and reduce the drying time. With good circulation, the drying process should take about an hour.

Preparing your image

You will need a solid black image on a transparency to prevent light from hardening the emulsion where you want your image to print. Don't invert or reverse the image. The best method is to print a digital image onto a transparency with a laserjet printer. You can also use an inkjet printer, but with these you may need to double up your transparencies to make them dark enough to block the light. You can also draw your image with paint pens or graphic pens that use lightfast ink. Stay away from Sharpies! They are not lightfast. You can use transparency paper for the transparency, but anything translucent will work: plastic, vellum paper, and even oiled copy paper (but oil it *after* it goes through the printer).

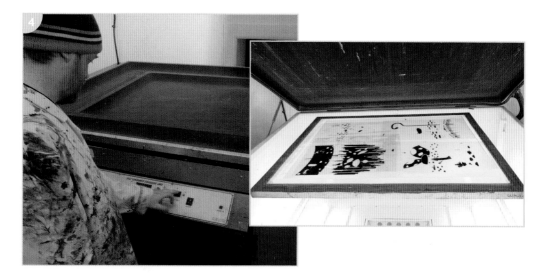

Exposing (or "burning") the screen

When the emulsion on your screen has dried, place the transparency face-up in the center of the glass on the exposure unit. You can use a little double-sided tape to secure two corners on the screen to align it, but make sure you can remove it quickly after exposure. Place the screen flat-side down on the transparency. The top of the image should be parallel to the top of the screen, with a good margin on all sides. Close and latch the lid, then turn on the vacuum switch. Place a weighted board inside the screen over the rubber cover.

When the vacuum is at its strongest, set the timer knob for three minutes. The lights will turn on and off again after the three minutes have elapsed. When the lights click off, turn off the vacuum and remove the board. Open the exposure unit and remove the transparency from the screen.

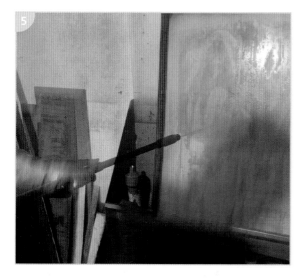

Washing the screen

Take the screen to the sink immediately to run/splash/spray water over every inch of emulsion on both sides. Turn the water off and take the screen outside to wash out. Use a pressure washer on a gentle setting, a hose, or a shower sprayer to wash both sides of the screen until the emulsion has been completely removed from the image area. Check this is done thoroughly by holding the screen up to a light source; the light should come through all parts of the screen. If there are any blockages, no matter how small, keep washing. Allow the screen to dry completely before attempting to print.

Preparing to print

Tape all the edges inside the screen. If you are using masking or packing tape, remember to remove it as soon as you have finished printing or you will have a sticky mess. Block off any parts of the screen that you don't want to print using tape or paper. Clamp your screen into your printing station, flat-side down. Center the image (unless you want it aligned otherwise).

Flooding

Apply a thin bead of ink to the screen behind the image. Without applying pressure, use the squeegee to pull the ink across the image until it is completely covered.

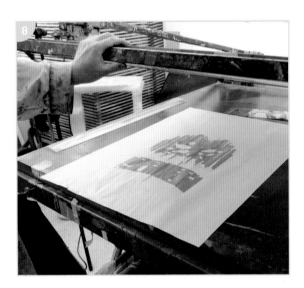

Printing

Hold your squeegee in both hands, angled slightly toward yourself. Apply pressure so that you feel its edge make contact with the surface below. Pull the squeegee firmly across the image. Repeat to ensure that all of the ink has been transferred to the surface. Pull up the screen to check, and reprint as necessary. Always pull a test print first.

Heat-set the image by drying it under a flash dryer or heat gun. Water-based inks can be left to dry, then turned inside out and run through a clothes dryer on high heat for about 45 minutes.

Clean up

Scrape up as much wet ink as possible and return it to the container for reuse. Wash the screen under running water and use a rag or sponge to remove any dried ink. Spray the image area until every bit of ink is removed and no scum is left on the open screen. Hold the screen up to the light to check. Do this thoroughly now as, once dry, it will be almost impossible to remove.

1.

1. Mikey Burton's poster for one of Richard Buckner's concerts, screenprinted in three colors, draws heavily from both packaging and the handmade aesthetic.

2. Michael Lewis of Studio MIKMIK printed these badges and their packaging on a Print Gocco—a small, self-contained printer that offers a clean, quick, and easy means of screenprinting.

2.

SIMPLE BLOCK PRINTING

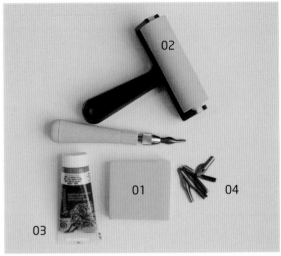

Carving and printing from a block is a great way to get your feet wet in the world of printing by hand. The supplies are cheap and the process is easy and fun. Block printing is also known as relief printing because you carve away the areas that you don't want to print from, leaving the image in relief. You can carve into wood, linoleum, or rubber block. For this tutorial, I used rubber block, which is very soft and easy to carve. A simple stamp such as this can be used to personalize muslin bags.

Materials
You'll need the following materials for block printing:
- a rubber, linoleum, or wood block (01)
- a brayer (02)
- ink: oil- or waterbased; for this tutorial, I used waterbased Speedball ink (03)
- a small sheet of plexiglass or glass
- carving tools (04)
- surfaces to print on (such as paper, fabric, or muslin bags)
- a kitchen spoon

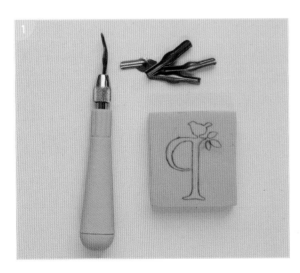

Creating and transferring your image
Start by drawing or transferring your image onto your block. To do this I printed out an image I created in Illustrator, then shaded a piece of tracing paper with my pencil and put the tracing paper on top of the block, shaded side down. I put my image on top of the tracing paper and traced it, thus transferring it to the block. Note that with this method, if you're using letters, text or numbers, they will need to be reversed on your block.

Carving your image
Carve away the areas of the block that you *don't* want to print: the areas left are what *will* print. I began by carving an outline around my letter with my smallest carving tool, then used a bigger carving tool on the larger areas. Always cut away from your design and your body; you don't want to cut yourself, or parts of your design that you need left intact.

Testing your print

Now create a test print to check how well your block prints. Squirt a blob of ink onto a nonporous surface such a piece of plexiglass or glass. Roll your brayer back and forth over the ink—you want just a thin, even coat of ink on it—then roll the brayer lightly over your block, taking care to ink only the areas of the block that are in relief. If it is difficult not to ink over other areas of the block, carve those down a little more. Create a test print on a sheet of paper. From the test print shown in the picture here, I could see that some areas around the edges of my block required further carving to create a better relief.

Printing

When you are satisfied with the quality of your test print, begin printing. There are various methods for this. The most obvious is to use the block like a rubber stamp. Lay the surface that will be printed on your work surface, position your inked block in the center, then press down hard. You may prefer to position your paper on top of the inked block and burnish the paper with a spoon. There isn't a right or wrong way to print, so experiment to discover what best suits your needs.

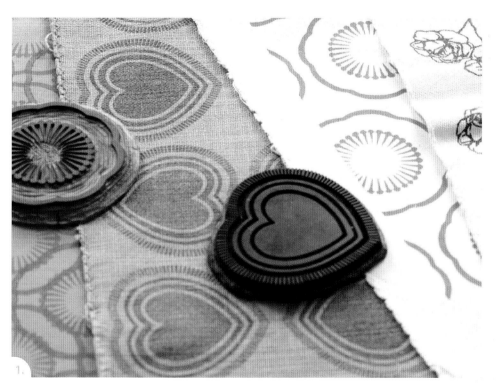

1. These fabrics, by Jesse Breytenbach, show how well small areas and lines work with block printing. Large areas can be broken up by cutting texture or patterns into them. (Photo: Warren Heath.)

CHAPTER 13 INDUSTRY ADVICE

If you want to apply your packaging designs to saleable products, the advice of the practitioners on the following pages offers insights into adapting the one-off and the small batch to a commercial scale without losing the appeal of the handmade.

SOMETHING'S HIDING IN HERE

The business began almost by accident. "A few years ago we decided to get a booth at the Renegade Craft Fair to raise enough money to buy a new computer. Let's just say, it worked! That weekend we bought a new computer and took our first wholesale order. The next week we set up an Etsy shop and have never looked back. We chose the name "Something's Hiding in Here" because we knew our product would evolve and we wanted a name that could grow with us without defining us too narrowly or too soon. We never intended to start a business and we refused to acknowledge it for a long time. We were afraid that it would lose the element of fun as soon as we took it too seriously. We were lucky to have made connections early on that quickly turned into friendships and nurtured our business along the way. From bloggers to shop owners, writers, photographers, and editors, we've been given so many amazing opportunities that helped our business grow organically."

Stephen Loidolt and Shauna Alterio of Something's Hiding in Here burst onto the indie scene with their handcrafted mustaches on sticks that became instantly ubiquitous. They spend a lot of time sewing their very popular Forage bow ties in their studio, which is located in an old Philadelphia tire factory. When they're not testing the limits of their sewing machine, they can still be found building things in their woodshop or printing on their Chandler & Price letterpress—which is also their primary resource for their packaging projects. "In the beginning we began packaging our goods out of necessity. Once we started our wholesaling to small shops, we recognized that our product needed packaging! It wasn't long before packaging became our favorite part, and now it's integrated into the product design from the beginning," says Shauna. "We love simple materials and always do our own printing. We spend more time, effort, and money on packaging than any rational business plan would suggest, but we love it."

1. Loidolt and Atlerio use printing tools and techniques that they are familiar with, and that they have to hand. For the boxes and tags shown here, they used letterpress and silkscreen printing.

> 56

For a case study of
Something's Hiding in
Here's tags, see page 56.

We love simple materials and do our own printing. We spend
more time, effort, and money on packaging than any
rational business plan would suggest, but we love it.

Stephen and Shauna find antique and vintage
printed goods a huge source of inspiration. "From
overly embellished turn-of-the-century sales slips
to graphic, mid-century brochures, our aesthetic
has become a mix of both old and new. We love to
think about the life of a product, from how it looks
in a photograph to how it sits on a shelf in a shop,
to how it looks when it's given as a gift."

The tools, methods, and processes that Stephen
and Shauna employ are lovingly selected and finely
honed. "We have favorite materials that we love to
work with and stick with them. We've been

collecting tools and growing our studio so that
we have the ability to keep everything in-house.
We really took this to the next level when we
acquired an old letterpress to print our packaging.
In addition to our Chandler & Price letterpress, we
rely on our antique guillotine paper cutter, an
old-school die cutter, and lots of butcher twine
and Kraft tag board."

For the would-be packaging designer, Stephen and
Shauna offer the following advice. "Keep packaging
humble and simple. Never force it to be more than
it needs to be."

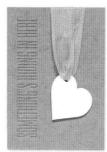

ERIC KASS

Eric Kass is a prolific artist and designer based in Indiana, USA. His work is incredibly distinctive and known for its handmade touch and aesthetic. You may have seen his work in 25-plus magazines, more than 40 books, over 30 gallery shows, or ricocheting around the Internet. He has many years of varied design experience, crafting award-winning, hard-working brands for a wide range of patrons around the globe, from start-ups to established endeavors, retail products, and unique services to the creative arts. In 2005 he founded Funnel: The Fine Commercial Art Practice of Eric Kass, a multi-disciplinary art and design studio in Indianapolis, Indiana.

Kass has a longstanding fascination with type. "In grade school I discovered different typestyles in the 'H' Worldbook Encyclopedia under Handwriting, for some reason. I would write love notes to pass in class the next day by drawing girls' names in black letter. They didn't necessarily swoon over my lettering skills but, looking back now, it was the beginning of my type fetish. My first job was summer help at a computerless design firm where I cleaned the stat camera and ran errands to pick up type from the typesetter. That's right, you actually had to go to a different company across town to pick up your type. We also used t-squares, triangles, French curves, toxic markers, amberlith, foam core, and razor-sharp knives. While at Ball State University, where I got a degree in Fine Arts, I worked for a printer, which was invaluable hands-on production experience. After school I had a variety of jobs from a large ad agency, a business-to-business marketing and design firm, a consumer-oriented design boutique, to my own small design firm that I started with a couple of partners. In 2005 I founded Funnel: The Fine Commercial Art Practice of Eric Kass (www.funnel.tv.)"

When describing his approach to design in general, Kass explains that "I am interested in developing stories that seduce, immerse, and instigate. I strive to create personal work that is engaging, memorable, and cherished. I do this by collaborating with amazing, inspiring, passionate patrons who allow me to artistically express their brand in strategically conceived, lovingly crafted commissioned work. I begin each packaging project by asking lots and lots of questions. What are we trying to say? What experience do we want to create for the customer? Where will this be sold? How will it ship? How will it be displayed? Why this product? Are there any legal regulations specific to this product's packaging? So on and so on."

Kass' inspiration comes from many sources, including "everything from musty printed ephemera, structured yet improvisational mid-century jazz, the emotional punch of Jackson Pollock, the melancholic wit of Charles Schulz, the wildly inspiring philosophies of Andy Warhol, the unashamedly naive typography usually found in back alleys or abandoned lots, trivia-inducing documentaries, scandalous biographies, often astoundingly accurate astrology, and the serene spirituality of ancient Eastern thought, especially wabi-sabi, the beauty of things imperfect, impermanent, and incomplete."

1.

For a case study of Eric Kass' recycled and upcycled packaging, see page 120.

1. Production costs for the labeling of this scented candle range were kept down by printing with just one ink. The second color was added by hand stamping, which also allowed the one label to be "personalized" for every scent in the range.

Many methods and processes can be seen in Kass' work. "I have used a little bit of everything, including letterpress, engraving, offset litho, screenprinting, and rubber stamps. I enjoy the methods that alter the surface dimensionally, like engraving or letterpress; or texturally, like screenprinting or rubber stamps. Combining materials and processes to create a variety of interactive textures is wonderful." When it comes to his design practices, he finds it useful to stick to certain processes. "Once the design story and direction has been developed, I always make a full-size mock-up to determine exactly how it feels in the hand and looks on the shelf. I even take it to a store to see how it looks in the actual marketplace with other products."

For Kass, the element or aesthetic of handmade is very important in his designs. "The imperfections, irregularities, and idiosyncrasies of hand-applied elements feel personal, human, and real in an increasingly digital world. A human, physical connection is extremely powerful in package design."

> I enjoy the methods that alter the surface dimensionally, like engraving or letterpress; or texturally, like screenprinting or rubber stamps.

Sustainability in packaging is interesting to Kass. "Packaging that can be reused for something else or can be discarded and decompose naturally is really intriguing. Bananas are packaged well. Avocados are amazing in how you can scoop out the insides, leaving only the thin, durable skin. I remember seeing something years ago where someone was experimenting with growing square fruits in a form that were easy to pack and left behind the logo in the skin. Interesting idea."

To aspiring package designers, Kass offers the following advice. "Understand and embrace the fact that the story, design, production, and function are all closely interrelated, making package design challenging but fascinating."

HAMMERPRESS

Hammerpress is a letterpress and design studio that started as a store in 1994 and has since grown to a decent-sized studio based in Kansas City, Missouri, USA. They specialize in custom invitations, identity and business card design and printing, letterpress posters, and art prints, and also have a full line of stationery products and greeting cards.

Creative Director Brady Vest explains how Hammerpress came about. "I started working under the name Hammerpress around 1992. I had a bunch of friends in bands around Kansas City and we started hand-printing the packaging for those bands. Once I graduated I began looking for equipment and made some really great finds that became the beginning of our collection of type and printing presses. At that point, the shop had its own location and began doing more work for design firms and other custom clients."

Hammerpress' first packaging project was for the band Giants Chair. Vest explains, "These guys were, and still are, close friends of mine, and they were a legendary post-punk band from Kansas City in the early and mid 1990s. We printed 500 CD packages and 500 vinyl packages for this project, all hand-silkscreened and printed on a hand-cranked Chandler & Price press (which has no motor or foot treadle). This was my favorite packaging project undertaken by Hammerpress. It was such a discovery process learning how and where to get a cutting die made, where to get some weird gray paper that we had a small little swatch of and driving all over Kansas City to find anyone who might know what it was."

Hammerpress vary their approach to design according to the client. "Both Anna Mae [see page 94] and Bearhouse [see page 92] were fantastic and lovely clients, but both very different. Because of the placement of the Anna Mae product and the amount being produced, we had to show much more finalized proofs of the designs for her to approve. Even though these designs were totally digital, most of the type and border/ornament materials were pulled from our collection in the print shop," explains Vest.

"The Bearhouse project required a very different approach. We sketched out some ideas—pencil sketches showing composition and placement— and created a mood board of sorts showing other projects we've done that have a similar feel. We discussed what kinds of decorative materials would be used, which kinds of paper, colors, etc. At that point, we got approval and started placing these pieces on the press bed. Once we got approval on the first color, we started printing. Then we moved on to the second, third, and fourth colors in the same way. This process is much more hands-on and organic, and labor-intensive."

Our concerns at Hammerpress are how to partner materials and aesthetics to fit both the needs and the idea of the project.

For case studies of Hammerpress' film and food packaging, see pages 92 and 94.

Vest finds inspiration for his designs in his collections of vintage packaging, postcards, matchbooks, stamps, records, ticket stubs, and other vintage ephemera. "Our concerns at Hammerpress are how to partner materials and aesthetics to fit the need of the project, but also the idea of the project. I grew up buying records and was always attracted to the object itself before ever experiencing what was on the record. Beyond the personal client concerns, our goal is to always make something feel real and authentic and, hopefully, like something that could have been made 50 years ago or last week."

While the team at Hammerpress have experimented in working with outsourced processes in order to introduce a variety of methods into their work, they prefer to do the work themselves, and stick to what they do best—letterpress printing. "The Anna Mae project was a huge leap of faith for the client as well as us. This was the first time we had such a large job on a pre-made package that we had no experience with. Our main production pressman, Eric, made this project happen. His experience on the Heidelberg press was invaluable on this. Those are the exciting projects to us—seeing huge stacks of boxes full of blank bags turn into huge stacks of letterpress-printed bread bags."

1. To convey the idea of "heritage" for this family-recipe-based product, Hammerpress combined old wood type and lead ornaments with letterpress printing.

STITCH DESIGN CO.

Amy Pastre and Courtney Rowson, two graphic designers with a knack for hands-on design, joined forces in 2009 to create a full-service design company, Stitch Design Co. based in Charleston, South Carolina, USA. They offer custom tailoring for design projects large and small.

After a degree in Graphic Design, Pastre moved to Charleston from Miami to begin her professional career, gaining experience at a newspaper agency, and a small design firm. Rowson attended the University of North Carolina at Chapel Hill and, after several years of working in design firms in Telluride, Colorado, and San Francisco, California, she worked independently before joining forces with Pastre.

Their first packaging project was for King Bean Coffee Roasters. "They are a small local coffee roaster supplying coffee to restaurants. They initially came to us to rebrand them. Once we completed the rebrand, we moved into incorporating their new brand into the restaurant packaging and retail packaging. First and foremost, they wanted their products to reflect their experience and expertise in the Charleston coffee market. At the same time, they are a small company and we had a budget to stay within. For the restaurant line of packaging we designed a custom packaging tape and label system. Each of the bags were sealed with packing tape and finished with a customizable label. The retail line was a complement to the restaurant packaging, which was silkscreened with standard information and included a more detailed labeling system. This approach gave the final product a cost-effective solution, but also one that felt layered and customized," says Pastre.

Pastre and Rowson's design approach to packaging remains the same for most of their projects. "When it comes to packaging, what changes the most is the usability—making sure the packaging is not only smart, handsome, stands out from the crowd, and is on brand, but also functions properly. Before we start any project we do a lot of research, both visual and verbal. We meet with the client in person to hear about their goals for the packaging but also try to look and listen to the other cues they may give while we meet. We also ask our clients to share inspiration with us. What do they respond to visually? What don't they respond to visually? When doing our own research, we look to other areas of design the most for inspiration. Textile design, product design, and interior design are all areas of inspiration for us. Paper, materials, color, and printing process is the first place we start as we consider the end product from the beginning. How will it feel in your hand? How do we want the user to experience the design? How can we use paper and other materials to enhance our design direction? We try to answer all of the questions at the onset of the project. After the design phase is complete, we enter another phase, which includes testing and retesting the packaging to make sure it functions right for the product and the audience," says Pastre.

We want the users of our designs to smile, open their eyes a bit wider, and move their fingers over the packaging. Paper and materials are items we are drawn to. The handmade aesthetic just seems to present itself.

When it comes to inspiration, Pastre and Rowson look to the product itself and the existing brand. "We strive to capture the essence of the product and brand in the packaging. We're always looking for ways to make the packaging cost-effective, communicative, and attractive. And we always look to items of the past to inspire new designs. Looking at vintage type, patterns, and printing methods is often a place where we start the design process. We are always striving for that balance of looking to the past while still infusing our designs with a clean, modern aesthetic. Textiles, fashion, vintage books, food, interiors, blogs, travel ... there is so much out there to be inspired by and we try to find inspiration everywhere we go. Discovering new restaurants, visiting museums, exploring different landscapes, and checking out the local culture all seem to really fuel our creativity."

A range of printing methods have found their way into Stitch Design Co.'s work. "We have used offset printing, silkscreening, and letterpress. We often use a combination of printing processes, which is our ideal solution. Mixing papers and printing processes gives the final product depth and a truly unique look. Our background as print designers influences our approach to packaging. We find ourselves infusing that knowledge into the world of packaging, which we think is a good thing!"

The handmade aesthetic and elements also find their way into the work of Stitch Design Co. Pastre explains, "Experiential design is very important to Stitch. We want the users of our designs to smile, open their eyes a bit wider, and move their fingers over the packaging we've designed. Paper and materials are items that we are naturally drawn to. Our design approach seems to yield solutions that fit in this category. The handmade aesthetic just seems to be an aesthetic that presents itself."

When looking at current package design, Pastre and Rowson enjoy how designers are now catering to a more design-savvy audience. "In general, the consumer is becoming more and more aware of design and more and more aware of good design. This awareness has elevated packaging design. We love that we're seeing more people simplify not only the design but also the materials they use. Less waste, better design."

To aspiring packaging designers, Stitch Design Co. say, "Take your time. You have to wear several hats when designing for packaging. You have to consider budget, design, and function. Packaging is complex, so give yourself ample time to work through the design and test multiple solutions."

1.

For case studies of Stitch Design Co.'s wrapping paper and upcycled packaging , see pages 108 and 116.

1. Stitch Design Co. used a layered labeling system for a range of candles not only to carry all the necessary information, but also to build up color, texture, and character.

DESIGNBRIDGE

DesignBridge is an international branding agency that creates, revives, and develops consumer and corporate brands. Founded in 1986, DesignBridge offers integrated brand solutions with expertise in innovation, brand strategy, brand identity, and brand packaging. The agency works across 50 different countries worldwide for brands such as Unilever, TNT, Sara Lee, Kraft, and Cadbury, from offices in London, Amsterdam, and Singapore.

One of DesignBridge's earliest projects was to redesign Bulmer's Woodpecker Cider, a classic, well-loved British brand. Graham Southern, a Group Creative Director, explains, "I wanted to bring the woodpecker character to life and reflect a cheeky personality. I commissioned illustrator Diz Wallis to capture the bird pecking into the label and cider. I think it still stands the test of time 25 years later, although the typography is very of its time!"

The company's design process is based on carefully devised principles. Southern says, "We approach any project in the same way—we have a creative philosophy that all work is judged against, five points that summarize a DesignBridge Big Idea. It is:

- simple but bold;
- authentic to the brand;
- warm and engaging;
- brilliantly executed and crafted; and
- enduring and memorable.

"Digging deep to understand the truth and personality of the brand is crucial to us, to be authentic and unique to the brand to capture people's attention and really emotionally connect. I was always inspired by classic packs like Gitanes and how a small box can sum up the essence of a gypsy dancing in a smoky nightclub in the Pigalle, and the fact that the designer's name, M. Ponty, was featured on the pack. Commercial art that seduces you—I am still guided by this essence. All our work is judged by our creative philosophy so we can make sure we bring the brief to life."

For me the importance of handmade elements
is that they give the package depth and uniqueness—
a distinct personality.

For a case study of DesignBridge's food packaging, see page 96.

1. This clever design elevates a simple brown paper bag to an emotive and elegant package. The heart logo, formed by the figure 2 and a mirror-image of itself, not only carries the name of the product, but also conveys the number of base flavors and the warmth associated with home baking.

When it comes to DesignBridge's methods and processes, Southern asserts that "Attention to detail and finish is crucial to us. I encourage designers to use tactile and unique solutions. It is very rare that our work does not include bespoke and handcrafted elements. Depth and authenticity is crucial, but each project has to be different and, also, appropriate. Execution is vital—we work with excellent print consultants who push and challenge methods to realize the most stunning results."

The handmade aesthetic is an important part of the work produced by DesignBridge. "For me, the importance of handmade elements is that they give the package depth and uniqueness—a distinct personality. I believe strongly in encouraging craft skills and we have regular guests and run workshops to develop these skills in our studios."

Contemporary packaging is something Southern finds exciting and inspiring. "I think we are emerging from a period in which packaging has been viewed as somewhat of a commodity. Today, I am seeing some bold ideas-driven work with a commitment to detail from around the world. There is fantastic work starting to come from emerging markets. As a judge on a recent packaging awards panel I found that the most striking work was from the most unusual places."

Southern would advise aspiring packaging designers to "be curious. Don't follow trends or fads; be timeless. Don't look at things on your screen—dress and play with the packaging. Don't over-complicate or lose the big idea. Always be open to 'What if?' Sometimes, those magic moments come right at the end of a project."

ILOVEDUST

ilovedust is a multidisciplinary design boutique. They specialize in creative solutions from graphic design and illustration to animation and trend prediction. They ply their trade in two contrasting studio spaces; one located in the heart of East London, England, UK, the other on the south coast of England, in Southsea, Hampshire. "The blend of both environments provides us with a unique and inspiring perspective," explains Partner Mark Graham. They collaborate both in-house and with global brands to create fresh, innovative designs.

The company was founded by Mark Graham and Ben Beach in 2003. "We had met each other while working at a Bournemouth-based clothing label and had struck up a good friendship that resulted in conversations about doing our own thing and doing something better than what we were working on at the time. ilovedust was born of frustration but also, I think, born out of a desire to do something new," says Graham.

Their first packaging project was for Breuckelen gin. "We desperately wanted to work on some packaging so I had emailed all the cool micro breweries around to see if anyone needed anything. Breuckelen came back and pretty much said we could do what we liked as long as it was one-color and we included his dog in the artwork!"

ilovedust's approach to design is very much a collaborative affair. "I think we look at something from two or three different directions; our studio is a nice size so we can get various ideas and aesthetics from different designers. Doing this allows us to work on a variety of products and packaging without being pigeonholed by one or two distinctive looks. I think the way we work is somewhat different to studios that do a majority of packaging or specialize in it. We admittedly are not experts so we find the best way to work is to push the boundaries of what is possible and let the client reel us in. This keeps things exciting and not so formulaic."

Having something that adds quality to packaging is important. Using a handmade aesthetic is one way to add warmth and depth to an idea. A certain tactile quality and interest can be obtained if you do it right and that is something we really believe in.

For a case study of ilovedust's box designs , see page 68.

1. ilovedust wanted a strong handmade aesthetic for its "vegetable-plot-in-a-box" to reflect the hands-on nature of gardening.

When it comes to design methods and practices, ilovedust like to keep on their toes. "Pushing away from what you know and mixing it up a little, I think, would be the only real practice we would try to adhere to. With a team of such good graphic designers and illustrators we try hard to create something new. Letterpress is always fun, and screenprinting is something we all scramble to do. Being hands-on to create solutions is something that is very satisfying. We are also starting to use customization more and more; with digital printing techniques allowing multiple content, it has opened up a whole new thought process to explore. There are so many great and inspiring things being created right now. That drives us—to want to be a part of that. Different printing techniques and materials are popping up almost daily and that alone is reason to keep rethinking what can be done."

Graham believes the handmade aesthetic can add value to a project. "Having something that adds quality to packaging is of the utmost importance to any product. Using a handmade aesthetic is one way to make an idea have more warmth and depth to it. A certain tactile quality and an interest can be obtained if you do it right and that is something we really believe in."

Graham advises aspiring packaging designers to "push yourself, push your client, and look at what has gone before you. Many ideas and aesthetics have changed over the years, but revisiting the past can be as exciting as looking to the future."

RESOURCES

GLOSSARY

MATERIALS

art paper
See Coated stock.

cartonboard
A fiber-based material of varying weights used extensively in consumer packaging for its excellent structural and printing properties.

coated stock
A smooth, hard-surfaced paper good for reproducing halftone images. It is created by coating the surface with china clay.

corrugated board
Highly ridged board made up of layers of flat and corrugated paper for excellent strength and rigidity. Often used for primary packaging.

crown cork
The metal closure, usually with rubber insert on the underside, used to seal the tops of glass bottles.

folded boxboard
See Cartonboard.

heat-shrunk sleeves
Preprinted plastic film applied over the surface of a container and then heated to shrink over the surface, completely enveloping it and creating a permanent label.

high-density polyethylene
A high-tensile thermoplastic used extensively in the packaging industry for uses ranging from plastic bags to rigid containers.

low-density polyethylene
Very tough thermoplastic used in a wide range of packaging applications from connector rings for multipack drinks cans to coating containers in order to provide a transparent barrier protection.

metallized film
Laminated film composed of layers of plastic and metal. The metal film provides either decorative (shiny effect) or functional (barrier protection) properties.

oriented polypropylene labeling (OPP)
Strong and moisture-resistant plastic labeling that can be applied at high speeds in cut-and-stack and, specially, reel-fed processes.

polyethylene terephthalate (PET)
Thermoplastic used extensively in the bottling industry for its strength and barrier properties.

polypropylene
A flexible plastic sheet available in many different colors, including clear and frosted.

pressure-sensitive labeling
Labels produced with three layers: paper, transparent adhesive, and backing. When the backing is removed and pressure is applied, the labels will adhere to most surfaces.

pulpboard
Uncoated board made from wood pulp.

shrink-wrap film
A clear plastic film that is heated so that it shrinks and seals around a product or container to form a tight-fitting layer.

stock
Another word for the paper or board used to produce a design.

uncoated stock
Paper that has a rougher surface than coated paper, so it is both bulkier and more opaque.

vinyl labeling
Plastic adhesive material, available in many colors.

PRINTING

bespoke Pantone colors
Colors created by mixing inks together to form an individual color that does not appear on Pantone referencing charts. *See also* Pantone.

CMYK
See Full color.

ceramic labeling
Application of ceramic inks directly onto the surface of a glass bottle through a screenprinting process.

duotone
Where two colors are printed together to make an image richer and denser in color.

full color
Almost all mass-produced print uses litho-graphic inks. As a rule, full-color printing is achieved through the combination of four process colors: cyan, magenta, yellow, and black/key (CMYK).

full-color black
Black created by combining cyan, magenta, and yellow inks.

Gocco
A screenprinting system using flash bulbs, a photocopy or carbon-based image, and an emulsion-coated screen. When the bulbs are manually flashed, the carbon in the photocopy or drawing burns the screen into a stencil. Several colors of ink can then be applied at one time and multiples can be stamped out before re-inking is needed.

halftone
A process used to reproduce an illustration, which involves breaking it up into small dots of different densities to simulate a full tonal range.

holographic
An image made with a split laser beam that, when suitably illuminated, shows a three-dimensional image.

Metallix printing system
A printing system that does not require the use of metallized inks. Colors and metallic effects are built up using stochastic and halftone screening for different print elements, together with two registered varnishes, achieved inline.

offset lithography
A method of printing using plates with image areas attracting ink and nonimage areas repelling it. Nonimage areas may be coated with water to repel the oily ink or may have a surface, such as silicon, that repels ink.

Pantone
An international professional color-matching system, which includes colors created out of the four-color set, "special" individual colors, metallics, fluorescents, and pastels.

Pantone special
The term referring to a specific color recipe created by Pantone and described by a name or number.

process colors
See Full color.

screenprinting
A printing method that applies ink to the surface of the material with a squeegee through a fine silk mesh. This achieves a much denser application of ink than lithography and may be used on a huge variety of surfaces.

spot color
A special color not generated by the four-color process method.

tritone
Where three colors are printed together to make an image richer and denser in color.

two passes of ink
Printing the same color twice, with the second pass of the press printing directly over the first to create a deeper, more intense, result.

vegetable-based inks
Inks that are made with vegetable-based oils—as opposed to mineral-based, such as petroleum—and that are, as a result, more environmentally friendly.

web-fed press
Printing press that prints onto a continuous roll of paper or plastic film. Printing is fast and can be applied to both sides of the material at once.

FINISHING

cut-and-stack labeling
Conventional method of labeling that delivers labels from a series of stacked flat sheets. Slower than the more modern and versatile reel-fed process.

cutting form
See Die-cutting.

debossing
Having a surface pattern pressed into the surface of the material. This process is also known as blind embossing.

die-cutting
The method by which intricate shapes can be cut from cartonboard. This process requires a custom-made die, which has a sharp steel edge constructed to cut the required shape.

embossing
Having a raised surface pattern. This is created by pressing the packaging material between a male and female form.

etching
The process of marking a metal or glass surface by corrosion, usually acid.

foil blocking
See Hot-foil stamping.

hot-foil stamping
Application of heat and metallic film in a specialty printing process that produces a shiny design on paper, vinyl, textiles, wood, hard plastic, leather, and other materials. Foil stamping is also called hot stamping, dry stamping, foil imprinting, or leaf stamping.

lamination
The application of a clear matte or gloss protective film over the printed surface of a sheet of paper or card.

laser cutting
A process that produces intricate cutting through most materials using a laser beam.

reel-fed labeling
A process of applying labels to containers from a reel. Delivered at high speed, this process allows a low-cost solution with superior optical qualities.

"soft-touch" varnish
A varnishing effect that has a light sponginess, leaving a slight softness on the surface to which it is applied.

spot varnish
See UV varnish.

UV varnish
A plastic-based varnish applied by screen-printing, available in matte, satin, and gloss finishes. It can be applied over the entire surface or treated as a spot varnish, enabling the designer to print elements purely as a varnish or to highlight selected elements on the page.

USEFUL WEBSITES

GUIDES

Packaging logistics
www.packagingprice.com
www.packstrat.com
www.sustainablepackaging.org

Shipping logistics
www.iship.com
www.intershipper.com

Gocco printing
www.savegocco.com

Letterpress printing
www.briarpress.org
www.fiveroses.org/intro.htm

Screenprinting
www.silkscreeningsupplies.com

MATERIALS

Bottles, bags, and boxes
www.associatedbag.com
www.clearbags.com
www.ebottles.com
www.muslinbag.com
www.packagingsupplies.com
www.specialtybottle.com
www.uline.com

Fabrics and papers
www.molded-pulp.com
www.nashvillewraps.com
www.papermart.com

Labels and tags
www.uline.com

Tools and equipment
www.dickblick.com
www.hobbylobby.com
www.silkscreeningsupplies.com

INSPIRATION

www.thedieline.com
http://lovelypackage.com
www.packagingoftheworld.com
http://packaginguqam.blogspot.com
www.spoonflower.com
www.sustainablepackaging.org

CONTRIBUTORS

Abby Brewster
http://cargocollective.com
abbybrewster

Aesthetic Apparatus
(Dan Ibarra and Michael Byzewski)
http://aestheticapparatus.com

Anoria Gilbert
(Maak Soap)
www.maaksoaplab.com

Atipus Design
www.atipus.com

Atolon de Mororoa
(Andres Amodio)
www.atolondemororoa.com

Benign Objects
(Rachel Wiles)
http://benignobjects.blogspot.com

Bethany Wuerch
http://wakeworkrinserepeat.
blogspot.com

Camille Deann
www.camilledeann.com

Chelsea Hendrickson
www.chelseahendrickson.com

Chen Design Associates
www.chendesign.com

Chewing The Cud
(Viola Sutanto)
www.chewingthecud.com

Chris Chapman
http://cjchapmandesign.co.uk

Chris Piascik
http://chrispiascik.com

Corrupiola
http://corrupiola.com.br

David Arias
http://arias.ca

Delphine Press Studio
(Erika Firm)
http://delphinepress.com

Denise Franke
www.dfact.de

Depot WPF
(Ekaterina Lavrova)
www.depotwpf.com

DesignBridge
(Stephanie Prentice)
www.designbridge.com

Dever Elizabeth
http://deverelizabeth.com

Devers Ink & Lead
(Wade Devers)
www.wadedevers.com

Duncan/Channzon
(Jennifer Moe)
www.duncanchannon.com

Elea Lutz
www.nostalgiaorganics.com

Elegante Press
(Viktorija Dumbliauskiene)
www.elegantepress.com

Eric Kass
www.funnel.tv

France Wisniewski
http://bananafishstudio.com

Francisca Aldea Davila
http://franaldea.blogspot.com

Frank Aloi
http://frankaloi.com.au

Freddy Taylor
www.freddytaylor.co.uk

Freshthrills
www.freshthrills.com

Funnel
(Eric Kass)
www.funnel.tv

Gen Design Studio
www.gen.pt/flash

Hammerpress
http://hammerpress.net

Heather Nguyen
www.heathernguyen.ca

Heydays
http://heydays.no

ilovedust
http://ilovedust.com

Insite Design
(Barry Imber)
http://insitedesign.ca

Jesse Breytenbach
www.jessebreytenbach.co.za

Jesse Harris
www.jesseharris.co.uk

Jessica Packard
www.jessicapackard.com

Joanna Kee
comehomesoap@hotmail.com

Josh Gordon Creative
www.joshgordoncreative.com

Khadia Ulumbekova
http://cargocollective.com/xx-xy

Kristen Magee
http://papercrave.com

Lauren Rogers
www.laurenrogers.com.au

Leonardo Di Renzo
www.typuglia.it

Lindsay Perkins
www.lindsayperkins.com

Little & Company
(Katie Watson)
www.littleco.com

Lorena Mondragon Rodriguez
http://cargocollective.com/lmondragon

Lucy King
www.lucykingdesign.com

Maak Soap Lab
(Lucy King)
www.maaksoaplab.com

Mads Jakob Poulson
www.madsjakobpoulsen.com

Mangion & Lightfoot
(Matthew Mangion & Mark Lightfoot)
www.mangionlightfoot.com

Mash Design
www.mashdesign.com.au

Matt Ellis
http://mattellis.com

Mikey Burton
www.mikeyburton.com

Miller Creative
(Yael Miller)
www.yaelmiller.com

Mind Design
(Holger Jacobs)
www.minddesign.co.uk

Nadia Arioui Salinas
http://nadia-arioui.blogspot.com

Office
(Julie Dyer)
www.visitoffice.com

Old Tom Foolery
lauren@oldtomfoolery.com

One Trick Pony
www.otpstudio.com/contact.html

Owen & Stork
www.owenstork.com

Pearlfisher
(Nellie Veltman)
www.pearlfisher.com

Peg & Awl
(Margaux and Walter Kent)
http://pegandawlbuilt.com

Perky Bros
(Jefferson Perky)
www.perkybros.com

Peter Gregson Studio
www.petergregson.com

Popular
office@popular.rs

Project Party Studio
(Daniel Horacio Agostini)
www.projectpartystudio.com

Rockit Science Agency
(Josh Dickerhoof)
rockitscienceagency.com

Samantha Schneider
www.wix.com/srschnei/samantha4

Skinny LaMinx
(Heather Moore)
http://skinnylaminx.com

Smith & Milton
(Rosie Milton)
www.smithandmilton.com

Something's Hiding In Here
www.somethingshidinginhere.com

Spoonflower
www.spoonflower.com

Stitch Design Co.
www.stitchdesignco.com

Stuart Kolakovic
www.stuartkolakovic.co.uk

Studio Boot
(Edwin Vollebergh)
www.studioboot.nl

Subplot Design Inc.
(Roy White)
www.subplot.com

Summer Watkins
http://summerwatkins.com

Susie Kirkwood
http://susiekirkwood.com

Tandem Design
(Eric Campbell)
www.tandemthinking.com

The Dieline
www.thedieline.com

Three Blind Ants
(Aaron and Ami Opsal)
www.threeblindants.com

Tubbyphunk
(Robert Page)
www.tubbyphunk.com

Twig & Thistle
(Kathleen Ullman)
www.twigandthistle.com

Typoretum
www.typoretum.co.uk

Vadim Paschenko
http://vadimpaschenko.com

Viola Sutanto
www.chewingthecud.com

Wallnut
(Cristina Londono)
http://wallnutstudio.com

Yujo! Creatividad Aplicada
(Joel Gutierrez Rodriguez)
www.yujo.com.mx

Zoo Studio
http://zoo.ad

PACKAGING CHART

		PACKAGE CONTENT		
		DRINKS	PERISHABLES	STORE-CUPBOARD
PACKAGING MATERIAL	GLASS	• pp. 30–33, 36, 38–39, 41–43, 50–51, 53, 62 • *in card outer* pp. 31, 37, 82, 118–119 • *in net outer* p. 37 • *in bubblewrap outer* p. 37 • *in wood outer* p. 53	• pp. 79, 124 • *in card outer* pp. 79, 82 • *with paper wrap* pp. 104–105	• pp. 26–27, 46–47, 51–52, 54–55, 58–59, 66, 121 • *with paper outer* pp. 51, 58–59 • *with wood outer* p. 87
	PLASTIC		• pp. 96, 125 • *in card sleeve* p. 109	• pp. 48–49, 55, 59, 95 • *in card outer* pp. 118–119
	PAPER		• pp. 28–29, 52, 96–97, 100–101, 124 • *in card sleeve* p. 112	• pp. 55, 96–99
	CARD	• *with glass jar* pp. 31, 37, 82, 118–119	• pp. 53, 55, 68–69, 74–75, 83–85, 87, 118–119 • *in fabric outer* p. 101 • *with glass jars* pp. 79, 82	• pp. 51, 78, 86, 118–119, 125 • *with glass jar* p. 59
	TIN	• p. 50		
	WOOD	• *with glass jar* pp. 53, 83	• *with glass jar* p. 87	• *with glass jar* p. 87
	FOAM			
	FABRIC	• *with glass jar* p. 113	• p. 55 • *with card insert* p. 101	• p. 99

TOILETRIES	CLOTHING AND ACCESSORIES	ELECTRICAL GOODS	STATIONERY	MERCHANDISE
• p. 52 • *in wood outer* p. 83				• pp. 116–117 • *in fabric outer* p. 120
• p. 45			• *in bubblewrap* p. 71	
• pp. 34–35, 72–73, 84, 100–101, 112				• pp. 67, 88–89 , 112
• pp. 84, 86	• pp. 56–57, 83, 125	• p. 82	• pp. 66–67, 70, 76–77, 84, 106–107	• pp. 60–61, 66, 80–81, 92–93, 114–115, 120 • *in fabric outer* pp. 90–91
• pp. 84, 86				
• *with glass jar* p. 83			• p. 87	• pp. 64–65 • *with glass jar* p. 83
• pp. 122–123			• pp. 67, 113	• pp. 85, 108, 110–111, 113 • *with card inner* pp. 90–91

INDEX

ABOUT THE AUTHOR

Rachel Wiles is an artist, designer, and writer.
She adores packaging of all sorts, but especially
that with handmade elements.

A contributer to The Dieline.com, a highly respected
packaging blog, she also writes for a number of design
publications; maintains a small design studio—Benign
Objects (www.benignobjects.com)—that specializes
in small business branding, packaging, illustration,
and stationery; and sells her creations from her online
shop (http://www.etsy.com/shop/BenignObjects).

Rachel's blog (http://benignobjects.blogspot.com)
highlights design of all types. Rachel lives in southern USA.

ACKNOWLEDGMENTS

I'd like to sincerely thank all of the wonderful contributors
to this project (many of whom have become new friends),
who took time out of their very busy lives to share their
beautiful work and thoughtful insights, and without
whom this book wouldn't exist.

I'd also like to thank the amazing team at RotoVision
for giving me this opportunity and providing invaluable
guidance along the way.

My dear family is a constant source of support and
inspiration, and my husband is the brightest beam
of light in my life. For their love and laughter, I am
eternally grateful.

And finally, I'd like to thank my high-school English
teachers, Mrs. Linda Thomas—who did her best to make
me understand dangling participles and gerunds and
who encouraged my writing—and Mr. Lewis Cobbs, who
nurtured my life-long love for reading with his incredible
wealth of knowledge and amazing ability to get students
excited about literature of all sorts—even Shakespeare
and *The Odyssey*!

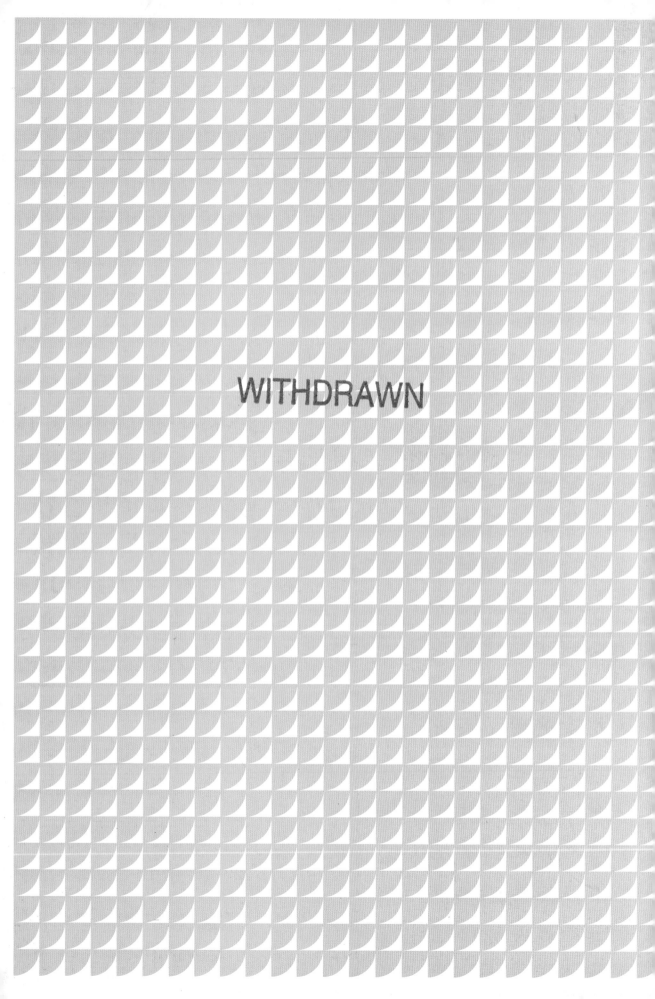

WITHDRAWN